FAMILY TREE
FACTBOOK

FAMILY TREE
FACTBOOK

Key Genealogy Tips and Stats
for the Busy Researcher

*Diane Haddad and the
Editors of Family Tree Magazine*

**FAMILY
TREE
BOOKS**

Cincinnati, Ohio | familytreemagazine.com/store

CONTENTS

Introduction

Maybe you're knee-deep in genealogy research at your local library when you come across a strange term. Maybe you're in a court records class and the instructor throws out an unfamiliar acronym. Or perhaps you're searching the census on Ancestry.com when you realize you need the census date to calculate your great-grandfather's age.

You could stop what you're doing and search for the right book or website to get the definition or date you need. Or you could pull out your handy *Family Tree Factbook*, look up what you need to know, and get on with your research.

We've gathered key resource lists, definitions, dates and other important reference information from *Family Tree Magazine* and FamilyTreeMagazine.com **<www.familytreemagazine.com>** and put it all into this handy guide. Keep it in your library tote bag or top desk drawer for easy reference.

HOW TO USE THIS BOOK

Check the table of contents to familiarize yourself with the information in this book. When you come across a genealogy word or acronym you don't know, need a statehood date, want to try a new website, wonder about the origin of a surname, have to calculate a Soundex code, need to know whether a family tree program is available for a Mac, want to learn how common your national heritage is, or need other pertinent information, just check the table of contents to find the appropriate chapter and section you need. Whenever your research uncovers a new resource or information that's pertinent to your family history, use the handy forms provided in the appendices. These forms are designed especially for you to record your favorite reference material and newly discovered information.

1

RESEARCH BASICS

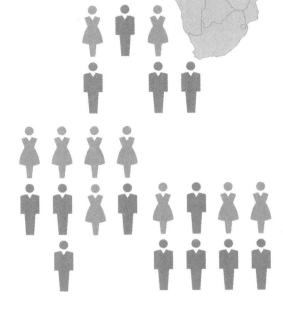

Genealogy Glossary

abstract: An abbreviated transcription of a document that includes the date of the record and every name in it; it may also provide relationships of the people mentioned.

admixture: Ancestry that originates from more than one ethnic group.

Ahnentafel: German for "ancestor table," this system of pedigree chart numbering gives each ancestor a number. Fathers are even numbers; mothers, odd. Double the child's number to get the father's (if you're 1, your father is 2). Add one to the father's number to get the mother's (your mother is 3).

aliquot parts: In the rectangular survey system, a description for a sub-division of a section of land using directions and fractions to indicate the land's location: *W½ SE¼* represents the west half of the southeast quarter of a township.

allele result: Also called a marker value, the numeric value assigned to a genetic marker.

ancestors: Relatives you descend from directly, including parents, grand-parents, great-grandparents and so on.

autosomal DNA: Genetic material inherited equally from mother and father, representing all your DNA except what's in the mitochondria and on the X and Y chromosomes. Autosomal DNA is the most widely used type of DNA in genealogy, as it can estimate ethnic origins and establish genetic relationships between test-takers.

banns (or **marriage banns**): Church documents publicly stating a couple's intent to marry.

block number: A one-, two-, or three-digit number that describes a block (or piece) of land within a township.

bond: A written, signed, and witnessed agreement requiring someone to pay a specified amount of money by a given date.

bounty land: Land granted by the Colonial and federal governments as a reward for military service; bounty land warrants—documents granting the right to the land—were assigned to soldiers, their heirs, or other individuals.

Bureau of Land Management General Land Office (GLO): The US government office historically in charge of dispersing public land. Usually, several branch land offices existed for each state; its website <**www.glorecords.blm.gov**> has a database with digitized federal land patents.

cemetery records: Records of those buried, as well as maps of grave sites; usually kept by cemetery caretakers.

census: An official count of the population in a given area; other details, such as names, ages, citizenship status and ethnic background of individuals, may be recorded. The US government has been collecting census data every ten years since in 1790. Many states have conducted their own censuses as well.

certified copy: A record copy made and attested to by custodians of the original who are authorized to give copies.

chromosome: A threadlike strand of DNA that carries genes and transmits hereditary information. Humans have forty-six chromosomes, organized into twenty-three pairs.

citation: The formatted information about a genealogical source that connects that source to each piece of family information it provides.

cluster genealogy: Studying your ancestor as part of a group of relatives, friends, neighbors, coworkers, and associates; this approach can help you learn details you might miss by looking only at records of an individual ancestor.

collateral relative: Any kin who aren't in your direct line, such as siblings, aunts, uncles, and cousins.

confidence range or **confidence interval**: Measure of how likely a result is to be accurate. A DNA results report shows the most likely ancestry percentages (for a biogeographic test) or date an MRCA lived (for a Y-DNA test), as well as a confidence range showing other possible results.

credit patent: A document transferring land to be paid for in installments over a four-year period. A delinquent payment or nonpayment of the full balance resulted in forfeiture.

declaration of intention: An alien's sworn statement that he or she wants to become a US citizen, also called "first papers"; these court records list details such as name, age, occupation, birthplace, and last foreign residence.

deed: A document transferring ownership and title of property; unlike a patent, a deed records the sale of property from one private individual to another.

derivative record: A document that has been copied, digitized, summarized, abstracted, extracted, indexed, transcribed, or otherwise created from another source. Try to track derivative records to the original. When you must use a derivative source, be sure to cite appropriately.

descendant chart: A report displaying names and information on a person's children, grandchildren, great-grandchildren, etc.

descendants: An ancestor's offspring—children, grandchildren, and every new generation in the direct line.

direct evidence: Information in a source that directly answers a research question. For example, if the research question was "What was his birth date?" then direct evidence of that answer would be a record stating the birth date as 12 May 1835.

DNA: The molecule that contains genetic code. Short for deoxyribonucleic acid; genetic genealogy tests analyze various types of DNA, especially Y-DNA, mtDNA, or autosomal DNA.

documentation: The process of citing sources of the family history information you've gathered, making it easier to keep track of the research you've completed and allowing others to verify your findings.

enumeration districts: Divisions of an area used to make census taking more efficient and accurate. For large cities, the boundaries of enumeration districts often match those of wards or precincts.

extract: A quoted passage taken from a source. Unlike an abstract, an extract isn't edited down to the bare essentials. An extract doesn't necessarily include key information from the entire document, just one passage.

family group record (or **sheet**): A worksheet that succinctly summarizes your information on a couple and their children; includes names; dates and places of birth, baptism, marriage, death and burial; and source citations.

Family History Center: A local branch of the FamilySearch library network. Each location contains a variety of digital and microfilmed records.

Family History Library (FHL): The world's largest collection of genealogical information, founded in 1894 by the Church of Jesus Christ of Latter-day Saints (LDS church). The main branch is in Salt Lake City, Utah. The FamilySearch website <**www.familysearch.org**> contains genealogical databases and the library's catalog.

five-generation ancestor chart: A family tree chart with five columns reading from left to right; this lists vital information for a person (in column 1) and his or her parents (column 2), grandparents (column 3), and so on.

freedman: A person released from slavery.

gazetteer: A geographical dictionary; a book giving names and descriptions of places, usually in alphabetical order.

GEDCOM: GEnealogy Data COMmunications, the universal file format for genealogy databases that allows users of different software programs to share family tree data with others.

gene: A hereditary unit consisting of a sequence of DNA that occupies a specific location on a chromosome and determines a particular characteristic in an organism.

Genealogical Proof Standard: A professional standard for credible research set by the Board for Certification of Genealogists. Its elements include a reasonably exhaustive search for answers, complete and accurate source citations, analysis and correlation of evidence, resolution of conflicting evidence, and a well-reasoned and well-written conclusion.

genealogy: The study of your family's history; the process of tracing your ancestors back through time.

genetic marker: A specific location on a chromosome where the basic genetic units exist in a variable number of repeated copies. DNA tests analyze a collection of genetic markers.

genotype: The compilation of multiple genetic markers; the unique genetic identifier for any given individual.

haplogroup: An identification of the genetic group your ancient ancestors (10,000 to 60,000 years ago) belonged to, sometimes referred to as a branch of the world's family tree.

haplotype: Collectively, the marker values on your Y-DNA or mtDNA test results.

home source: Sources of any kind you find from family members and in your or a relative's home. Though these sources may be fragmented or undocumented, they are more likely to be relevant to your family and not to others of the same name (a problem common to finding records outside the family).

homestead: A home on land obtained from the US government; the homesteader agreed to live on the land and make improvements, such as adding buildings and clearing fields.

Homestead Act of 1862: A law allowing people to settle up to 160 acres of public land if they satisfied certain requirements; the land was free, but the settler paid a filing fee.

HVR (hypervariable region): Sections of mtDNA (such as HV1 and HV2) used to determine your haplogroup.

index: In genealogical terms, a list of names taken from a set of records. For example, a census index may list the names of people recorded in a given area in the 1870, 1880, 1900, or another census. Indexes are often used in online databases and are also available in books and on CD, microfilm, and microfiche. They usually provide source information for the source records.

indirect evidence: Information that helps answer a research question but doesn't answer it in full. Let's say you're trying to identify Sadie's parents. One document links Sadie to her twin sister Alice and another gives Alice's parents' names. These two indirect pieces of evidence combine to answer your question.

informant: The person providing the information recorded in a document, as in a birth record. The reliability of the informant affects the accuracy of the evidence.

International Genealogical Index (IGI): A pedigree database on FamilySearch.org; contains roughly 250 million names either submitted to the church or extracted from records the church has microfilmed.

intestate: Describes a person who died without a will.

Julian calendar: The calendar used from 46 BC to 1582, named for Julius Caesar; it's often referred to as the "Old Style" calendar and was replaced by the Gregorian calendar.

kindred: Blood relatives.

land claim: A settler's application to receive public land.

land-entry case file: A file created when a person claimed land under an act of Congress, such as the Homestead Act of 1862; the person first filled out an application at the local General Land Office. The file might contain marriage, immigration, or other documents. Files are available from the National Archives and Records Administration.

land grant: Public land given to an individual by the government, usually as a reward for military service.

land patent: A document transferring land ownership from the federal government to an individual.

legacy: Property or money bequeathed to someone in a will.

legal land description: In a land patent, an exact identification of the land being transferred using survey terms.

lien: A claim placed on property by a person who is owed money.

local history: Usually, a book about the development of a town or county; these were popular in the late nineteenth century and often include details of the area's prominent families.

manuscripts: Private documents and records such as diaries, letters, family Bible entries, and organizations' papers; you can find manuscript collections through a search of the National Union Catalog of Manuscript Collections (NUCMC) library holdings.

medical records: Paperwork associated with medical treatments from hospitals, asylums, doctors, or midwives; may be considered private documents and inaccessible to the public.

meridian: An imaginary north-south line; a principal meridian is the starting point for a rectangular land survey.

metes and bounds: A land survey method employing compass directions, landmarks and distances between points.

military records: Records of military service kept by the federal government (from the Revolutionary War to the present) and state government (for state militias and guards); examples are service records, pensions, bounty land warrant applications, draft registration cards, and discharge papers.

Miracode system: An indexing system similar to Soundex used to organize the results of the 1910 census; the computer-generated cards are organized first by Soundex code, then alphabetically by county, then alphabetically by given name.

mitochondrial DNA: Genetic material mothers pass on to both male and female children. Because it's passed down relatively unchanged, mtDNA can reveal "deep ancestry" along your maternal line—but not definitive links to recent generations.

mortality schedule: A special federal census schedule listing persons who died during the census year.

MRCA (most recent common ancestor): The most recent ancestor two individuals descend from.

mutation: Change in DNA that spontaneously occurs. Mutations can reveal how long ago two individuals' MRCA lived.

National Archives and Records Administration (NARA): The United States' repository for federal records, including censuses, military service and pension records, passenger lists and bounty land warrants; in addition to the primary archives in Washington, DC, NARA has regional facilities across the nation.

negative evidence: When a record is not found where it should appear, providing evidence toward a conclusion.

New England Historical and Genealogical Register System: A genealogical numbering system showing an individual's descendants by generation. All children in a family get Roman numerals (i, ii, iii ...) and every child later listed as a parent also gets an Arabic numeral (2, 3, 4 ...). The system is named for the journal of the New England Historic Genealogical Society.

NGS Quarterly (NGSQ) system: A narrative report showing an individual's descendants by generation. It uses an alternative numbering system to the other reports. A plus sign indicates that a child appears as a parent in the next generation. The system is named for the journal of the National Genealogical Society.

oral history: A collection of family stories told by a family member or friend.

original record: A document in its original format, such as an actual death register or a diary. An original record may contain both primary information (the death date on a death certificate) and secondary information (on a death certificate, the deceased's birth date may have been provided by an informant who wasn't present when the person was born).

orphan asylum: An orphanage, or home for children whose parents have died.

passenger list: List of names and information about passengers who arrived on ships; submitted to customs collectors at every port by the ship's master. Passenger lists weren't officially required by the US government until 1820.

pedigree: List of a person's ancestors.

pension (military): A benefit paid regularly to a veteran or his widow for military service or a military service-related disability.

Periodical Source Index (PERSI): A print and online index to thousands of genealogy and local history periodicals published in the United States and Canada back to the 1700s; PERSI is a project of the Allen County Public Library in Fort Wayne, Ind., and available through Findmypast <www.findmypast.com>.

petition for naturalization: An alien resident's request to be made a citizen, often called "second papers" because it was submitted after filing a declaration of intention and fulfilling any residency requirements.

plat: A drawing showing the boundaries and features of a piece of property; in genealogy, a surveyor would have created such a drawing from a metes-and-bounds or legal land description.

pre-emption: The right of a settler to acquire property that he had occupied before the government officially sold or surveyed it.

primary information: Data reported by an informant who has firsthand knowledge of an event. For example, an attending physician or coroner may provide primary information about a person's death on her death certificate.

primary source: A record or other piece of data created at the time of a particular event; a primary source is always the original record—birth and death certificates are primary sources for those events. Note that an original record isn't always a primary source: For example, a death certificate isn't a primary source for birth information.

probate records: Documents related to administering a deceased individual's property; they may include an individual's last will and testament. Information varies, but may include the name of the deceased, his age at death, property, family members, and last place of residence.

provenance: The history of ownership of an item.

public land: Land originally owned by the federal government and sold to individuals.

Quaker: A member of the religious group called the Society of Friends; Quakers kept detailed records of their congregations, including vital statistics.

quarter section: In the rectangular survey system, one-fourth of a section of land, equal to 160 acres.

range: A row or column of townships lying east or west of the principal meridian and numbered successively to the east and to the west from the principal meridian.

real property: Land and anything attached to it, such as houses, buildings, barns, growing timber, and growing crops.

recombination: The process by which chromosomes cross and switch genetic material at conception.

rectangular survey system: The land survey method the US General Land Office used most often; it employs base lines, one east-west and one north-south, that cross at a known geographic position. Townships—each generally twenty-four square miles—are described in relation to the base lines. Townships are subdivided into sections.

secondary information: Data reported by an informant who does not have firsthand knowledge of an event. A deceased woman's son who is the informant on her death certificate and provides his mother's birth date is giving secondary information.

secondary source: A document created after an event occurred, such as a biography, local history, index, or oral history interview; original records can be secondary sources for information about earlier events (a death certificate is a secondary source for a birth date).

section: A division of land within a township that measures one square mile (640 acres)—about 1/36 of a township; sections were further subdivided into half-sections, quarter-sections, and sixteenth-sections, or into lots.

self-addressed, stamped envelope (SASE): Include an SASE when you request records from people and institutions.

SNP (single nucleotide polymorphism): Harmless mutations in autosomal DNA that can indicate where your ancient ancestors came from.

Social Security Death Index: An index of Social Security Death records; includes names of deceased Social Security recipients whose relatives applied for Social Security Death Benefits after their passing.

Soundex: A system of coding surnames based on how they sound, used to index the 1880 and later censuses; Soundex is useful in locating records containing alternate surname spellings. Soundex cards are arranged by Soundex code, then alphabetically by given name.

state land: Land originally owned by a state or another entity, rather than the federal government.

STR (short tandem repeat): A type of recurring DNA marker used to determine relationships between individuals.

testate: Describes a person who died with a will.

township: In a government survey, it's a square tract six miles on each side (thirty-six square miles); a name given to the civil and political subdivisions of a county.

tract: A parcel of land that isn't fully contained within a single section; tracts within a township are numbered beginning with 37 to avoid confusion with section numbers.

union list or **catalog**: A bibliography or catalog of materials held by multiple repositories, such as the National Union Catalog of Manuscript Collections, a finding aid for personal papers in institutions nationwide.

usury: Historically, all interest paid.

visitation number: On a 1910 Miracode index card, the house number of the indexed individual.

vital records: Official records with basic information about a person's birth, marriage and/or divorce date and place, and death date and burial place.

volume number: On a Soundex or Miracode index card, the number of the census volume with the indexed name.

voter registration: A list of registered voters for each state. Voter registration lists are sometimes the first public records of former slaves. Many states have microfilmed their lists.

will: A document in which a person outlines what should be done with his or her estate after death; the legal process to see that those instructions are carried out is called probate.

witness: A person who sees an event and signs a document attesting to its content being accurate; family members, friends, neighbors and business associates commonly witnessed documents.

X: What the signer of a document would often write if he couldn't write his name; a witness would typically label this "his mark."

X-DNA: Genetic material parents pass on to their children along the X chromosome. X-DNA is often tested as part of autosomal DNA tests.

Y-DNA: Genetic material fathers pass on to their sons along the Y chromosome. Y-DNA tests can confirm (or disprove) genealogical links through a paternal line.

Genealogy Acronyms

AAD: Access to Archival Databases, part of the National Archives and Records Administration (NARA) website

AAGG: African-American Genealogy Group

AAHGS: Afro-American Historical and Genealogical Society

ACPL: Allen County Public Library (in Fort Wayne, Indiana)

AGBI: American Genealogical-Biographical Index

AIC: American Institute for Conservation of Historic and Artistic Works

ALE: Ancestry Library Edition, a data service available through many public libraries

APG ("ap-jen"): Association of Professional Genealogists

BCG: Board for Certification of Genealogists

BLM: Bureau of Land Management

BYU: Brigham Young University (in Salt Lake City, Utah)

CG: Certified Genealogist

CGL: Certified Genealogical Lecturer

CMSR: Compiled Military Service Record

CWSS: Civil War Soldiers and Sailors System

DAR: Daughters of the American Revolution (also NSDAR: National Society Daughters of the American Revolution)

ED: Enumeration district, a geographical division defined for a US census

FEEFHS ("feefs"): Foundation for East European Family History Societies

FGS: Federation of Genealogical Societies

FHC: Family History Center, a branch of the Family History Library

FHL: Family History Library (in Salt Lake City, Utah)

FHLC: FHL catalog

FOIA: Freedom of Information Act

FTDNA: Family Tree DNA, a genetic genealogy company

FTM: Family Tree Maker genealogy software

GAR: Grand Army of the Republic, a network of organizations for Civil War Union veterans

GEDCOM ("jed-com"): Genealogical Data Communications, the computer file format for family tree data (.ged is the extension for these files)

GLO: Bureau of Land Management General Land Office

GOONS: Guild of One-Name Studies

GPS: Genealogical Proof Standard

HQO: HeritageQuest Online genealogy databases, offered through many libraries

IAJGS: International Association of Jewish Genealogical Societies

ICAPGen ("eye-cap-jen"): International Commission for the Accreditation of Professional Genealogists

IGI: International Genealogical Index, on FamilySearch.org

ISFHWE ("ish-wee"): International Society of Family History Writers and Editors

ISOGG: International Society of Genetic Genealogy

LOC: Library of Congress

MRCA: Most recent common ancestor, the most recent ancestor you share with another person

MTDNA: Mitochondrial DNA

NARA ("nar-uh"): National Archives and Records Administration

NEHGS (sometimes called "hiss-jen"): New England Historic Genealogical Society (in Boston)

NERGC: New England Regional Genealogy Conference

NGS: National Genealogical Society

NUCMC ("nuk-muk"): National Union Catalog of Manuscript Collections

OR: The Civil War reference *The War of the Rebellion: A Compilation of the Official Records of the Union and Confederate Armies*

PAF: Personal Ancestral File genealogy software

PALAM ("pal-am"): Palatines to America

PERSI ("per-zee"): Periodical Source Index to family history articles in US and Canadian magazines and journals

PRO: Public Record Office of the United Kingdom

Red Book: *Red Book: American State, County and Town Sources*

RM: RootsMagic genealogy software

SAR ("sar"): Sons of the American Revolution (also NSSAR: National Society, Sons of the American Revolution)

SCGS: Southern California Genealogical Society (in Burbank, California)

SCV: Sons of Confederate Veterans

SGGEE (sometimes pronounced "squeegee"): Society for German Genealogy in Eastern Europe

SMGF: Sorenson Molecular Genealogy Foundation, a genetic genealogy organization that has ceased operations

SUVCW: Sons of Union Veterans of the Civil War

UDC: United Daughters of the Confederacy

WDYTYA?: The genealogy television series *Who Do You Think You Are?* (can refer to NBC's/TLC's US version or BBC's British version)

WRHS: Western Reserve Historical Society (in Cleveland, Ohio)

Genealogy Abbreviations

abr abridged; abridgement

abs or **abst** abstract

abt about

acc according to; account; accompanied

adm or **admin** administrator, administration

aka or **als** also known as; alias

al alien

anc ancestor

appx appendix

B black (indicating race)

b born

bp or **bpt** baptized; birthplace

bu or **bur** buried

cem cemetery

CH or **ch** courthouse, children; church; chief; chaplain

chr christened

cir, **c**, or **ca** circa

conf confirmed

CW Civil War

d died

decd or **dec'd** deceased

div divorced

do or **DTo** ditto

dom domestic

f female

FR family register

gdn or **grdn** guardian

inf infantry

inhab inhabitant; inhabited

jud judicial

junr junior

lic license

liv living

m male or mulatto

m or **md** married

mil military

mo month

n negro

na naturalized

n.d. no date; not dated

nm never married

NS "New Style" calendar

obit obituary

OS "Old Style" calendar

poa power of attorney

pr parish register; proved or probated

RC Roman Catholic

reg register

res residence; research

ret retired

s son

s & h son and heir

s/o son of

srnm surname

t or **twp** township

unk unknown

unm unmarried

w widowed

20 Questions to Ask Your Relatives

Ask open-ended questions (rather than ones with yes or no answers) during oral history interviews, and focus on people's experiences, not just names and dates. Start your question list with:

1. What's your first memory?

2. Who's the oldest relative you remember (and what do you remember about him or her)?

3. How did your parents meet?

4. Tell me about your childhood home.

5. How did your family celebrate holidays?

6. How did you meet your spouse?

7. Tell me about your wedding day.

8. Tell me about the day your first child was born.

9. What were your favorite school subjects?

10. Tell me about your favorite teacher.

11. Tell me about some of your friends.

12. Describe your first job.

13. What did you do with your first paycheck?

14. What was your favorite job and why?

15. Who are some of your heroes?

16. Where were you when you heard that President Kennedy had been shot? (Add or substitute other important historical events.)

17. What is your experience with or opinion of computers? (Add or substitute other modern conveniences, such as televisions, microwaves and cell phones.)

18. Tell me about some of your favorite songs (also books, movies, and television shows).

19. Tell me about some of the places where you've been happiest.

20. What haven't we talked about that you'd like to discuss in the time we have left? (This is a good way to begin wrapping up the interview.)

Common Genealogical Errors

Ask these questions to spot inaccurate names, dates, and relationships in your family tree research:

1. Do all the dates make sense? Did someone accidentally type *1966* instead of *1866*?

2. Does the chronology for each family group make sense? Is a mom giving birth too young or too old? Is a man marrying at age twelve? Are children born at least nine months apart? Is a child being born after the mother is dead? Or is a child born before its parents?

3. When you find research showing a child in his parents' family group who was then carried forward as an adult, do the child's details (such as date and place of birth) match the adult information?

4. What sources did the compiler use? Did she consult original records, such as censuses, passenger lists, and deeds? Or did she rely on secondary sources (citing, for example, "World Family Tree," "Aunt Susie's notes," or "Ted's GEDCOM file") that might regurgitate erroneous information?

5. Does biographical information seem exaggerated and too good to be true?

6. Are conclusions faulty? Has a compiler misinterpreted a document because she doesn't understand the legal terms for a particular time period? What information is the compiler basing a parent-child relationship on?

Major Genealogical Societies

Afro-American Historical and Genealogical Society
<www.aahgs.org>

Association of Professional Genealogists
<www.apgen.org>

Federation of Genealogical Societies
<www.fgs.org>

Foundation for East European Family History Societies
<www.feefhs.org>

International Association of Jewish Genealogical Societies
<www.iajgs.org>

National Genealogical Society
<www.ngsgenealogy.org>

National Society, Daughters of the American Revolution
<www.dar.org>

National Society, Sons of the American Revolution
<www.sar.org>

New England Historic Genealogical Society
<www.americanancestors.org>

6 Genealogy Myths to Avoid

1. **You can buy your family crest**. Cups, wall hangings, and other family crest doodads are available online. But "families" don't have crests—rather, individuals do. Coats of arms must be granted, and to claim the right to arms, you must prove descent through a male line of someone to whom arms were granted.

2. **The 1890 census burned to a crisp**. Actually, it didn't—it was water-logged and lay around until some unknown person authorized its disposal. But a small fraction survived and is on NARA microfilm and in online census collections.

3. **Your whole family history is online**. If only! You can get lots of records online, including censuses, passenger lists, military records, and digitized books. But errors abound in online indexes, transcriptions, and family trees. At some point, you'll want or need to log off and go to the library. Repositories hold richly detailed, lesser-known records.

4. **You have famous ancestry**. Maybe you believe your ancestor was a Cherokee princess or George Washington. Many families have legends about famous kin, and of course they could be true—but stories tend to get embellished and even made up over time, so research them before passing them on as truth. You may have Cherokee blood, but there weren't any Cherokee princesses. George Washington can't be an ancestor because he never had children (though his wife, Martha, had children from her first marriage).

5. **The courthouse burned; all the records are gone**. But records caught in courthouse fires weren't always completely destroyed. Sometimes records survived, or copies had been sent to another office. Clerks may have also asked citizens for replacement copies of their records.

6. **Your ancestor's name was changed at Ellis Island**. Passenger lists were created at the port of departure, and the ship's master would give them to immigration officials at the arrival port. Ellis Island officials just checked the names on the list; they didn't change any names. Many immigrants changed their own names after arrival in an effort to sound more "American." See **<www.genealogy.com/88_donna.html>** for more information on immigrant name changes.

Old Handwriting Styles

Secretary, Court Hand or Gothic, 1600s: This is the most common script found in seventeenth-century materials, and it's reflected in the handwriting style of early English immigrants. You'll also see Mayflower Century script, which is a combination of the Secretary style with Italian and, by 1700, Roundhand script.

Italian, 1400s to 1700s: Also called italics, this style is characterized by rounded letter formations. Queen Elizabeth of England (1533–1603) used cursive Italian script.

Roundhand or Copperplate, 1700 to late 1800s: This style became popular as copybooks—self-teaching handwriting manuals—began to be printed by copperplate engraving. It's recognizable by thin upstrokes and thicker downstrokes. The *s* is formed by a long flourish that's easily confused with a *p* or an *f*.

Spencerian, 1865 to 1890: Characterized by flourishes, Spencerian handwriting reflected the feminine pursuits of the Victorian period. Writing was a slow process because of all the loops and the number of times the writer lifted the pen.

Palmer, 1880 to 1960s: Partially in reaction to the time-consuming Spencerian writing, Austin Palmer developed this method of plain, legible script more suited to the fast pace of business offices.

D'Nealian, 1965 to present: Many children learning to write today are taught this style. See <www.dnealian.com> for more examples.

How to Calculate Cousinhood

You know two people are related but you can't figure out how? Use the relationship chart and follow these steps:

1. Identify the most recent common ancestor of the two individuals with the unknown relationship.

2. Determine the most recent common ancestor's relationship to each individual (for example, grandparent, or great-great-grandparent).

3. In the topmost row of the chart, find the common ancestor's relationship to the first individual.

4. In the far-left column, find the common ancestor's relationship to the second individual.

5. Trace the row and the column from step 4 until they meet. The square where they meet shows the relationship between the two individuals.

The Most Recent Common Ancestor is person 1's ...

	Parent	Grandparent	Great-grand-parent	Great-great grandparent	3rd-great grandparent	4th-great grandparent	5th great-grandparent	6th-great grandparent
Parent	sibling	nephew or niece	grandnephew or -niece	great-grand-nephew or -niece	great-great grandnephew or -niece	third-great-grandnephew or -niece	fourth-great-grandnephew or -niece	fifth-great-grandnephew or -niece
Grand-parent	nephew or niece	first cousins	first cousins once removed	first cousins twice removed	first cousins three times removed	first cousins four times removed	first cousins five times removed	first cousins six times removed
Great-grand-parent	grand-nephew or -neice	first cousins once removed	second cousins	second cousins once removed	second cousins twice removed	second cousins three times removed	second cousins four times removed	second cousins five times removed
Great-great grand-parent	great-grand-nephew or -niece	first cousins twice removed	second cousins once removed	third cousins	third cousins once re-moved	third cousins twice removed	third cousins three times removed	third cousins four times removed
3rd-great grand-parent	great-great-grandneph-ew or -neice	first cousins three times removed	second cousins twice removed	third cousins once removed	fourth cousins	fourth cousins once removed	fourth cousins twice removed	fourth cousins three times removed
4th-great grand-parent	third-great grandneph-ew or -niece	first cousins four times removed	second cousins three times removed	third cousins twice re-moved	fourth cousins once removed	fifth cousins	fifth cousins once removed	fifth cousins twice removed
5th great-grand-parent	fourth-great grandneph-ew or -niece	first cousins five times removed	second cous-ins four times removed	third cousins three times removed	fourth cousins twice removed	fifth cousins once removed	sixth cousins	sixth cousins once removed

Genealogy Records Checklist

BUSINESS AND EMPLOYMENT RECORDS
- [ ] apprentice and indenture records
- [ ] doctors' and midwives' journals
- [ ] insurance records
- [ ] merchants' account books
- [ ] professional licenses
- [ ] railroad, mining, and factory records
- [ ] records of professional organizations and associations
- [ ] Social Security applications (SS5)
- [ ] company newsletters
- [ ] government patents

CEMETERY AND FUNERAL HOME RECORDS
- [ ] burial records
- [ ] grave-relocation records
- [ ] tombstone inscriptions

CENSUSES
- [ ] agriculture schedules (1850 to 1880)
- [ ] American Indian (special censuses)
- [ ] Civil War veterans schedules (1890)
- [ ] defective, dependent, and delinquent (DDD) schedules (1880)
- [ ] federal population schedules (1790 to 1930)
- [ ] manufacturing/industry schedules (1810, 1820, 1850 to 1880)
- [ ] mortality schedules (1850 to 1880, 1885)
- [ ] school censuses
- [ ] slave schedules (1850, 1860)
- [ ] social statistics schedules (1850 to 1870, 1885)
- [ ] state/territorial and local censuses

CHURCH RECORDS
- [ ] baptism and christening records
- [ ] confirmation records
- [ ] congregational histories
- [ ] marriage banns
- [ ] meeting minutes
- [ ] membership, admission, and removal records
- [ ] ministers' journals

COURT RECORDS

- ☐ adoption records
- ☐ bastardy cases
- ☐ civil records
- ☐ coroners' files
- ☐ criminal records
- ☐ custody papers
- ☐ estate inventories
- ☐ guardianship papers
- ☐ insanity/commitment orders
- ☐ licenses and permits
- ☐ marriage bonds, licenses, and certificates
- ☐ military discharges
- ☐ minute books
- ☐ name changes
- ☐ naturalizations
- ☐ property foreclosures
- ☐ voter registrations
- ☐ wills
- ☐ wolf-scalp bounties

DIRECTORIES

- ☐ biographical
- ☐ city
- ☐ professional/occupational
- ☐ telephone

HOME SOURCES

- ☐ baptism and confirmation certificates
- ☐ birth certificates and baby books
- ☐ checkbooks and bank statements
- ☐ death records and prayer cards
- ☐ diaries and journals
- ☐ family Bibles
- ☐ funeral/memorial cards
- ☐ heirlooms and artifacts
- ☐ letters and postcards
- ☐ marriage certificates and wedding albums
- ☐ medical records
- ☐ photographs
- ☐ recipe books

☐ school report cards, yearbooks, and scrapbooks
☐ wills

IMMIGRATION RECORDS
☐ alien registration cards
☐ citizenship papers (declarations of intention, certificates of naturalization)
☐ passenger lists
☐ passports and passport applications

INSTITUTIONAL RECORDS
☐ almshouses
☐ hospitals
☐ orphanages
☐ police stations and registers
☐ prisons
☐ schools
☐ work-farms
☐ fraternal associations

LAND AND PROPERTY RECORDS
☐ deeds
☐ grants and patents
☐ homestead records
☐ mortgages and leases
☐ plat maps
☐ surveys
☐ tax rolls
☐ warrants

MILITARY RECORDS
☐ Colonial wars
☐ Revolutionary War and frontier conflicts (War of 1812, Indian wars, and Mexican War)
☐ Civil War
☐ Spanish-American War
☐ World War I
☐ World War II
☐ Korean War
☐ Vietnam War
☐ draft records
☐ pension applications

☐ records of relocations and internment camps for Japanese-Americans, German-Americans and Italian-Americans during World War II

NEWSPAPERS
☐ birth announcements
☐ classified advertisements
☐ engagement, marriage, and anniversary announcements
☐ ethnic newspapers and immigrant ship notices
☐ family reunion announcements
☐ gossip and advice columns
☐ legal notices
☐ local news
☐ obituaries/death notices
☐ runaway notices (slaves, indentured servants, wives)
☐ unclaimed-mail notices

PUBLISHED SOURCES
☐ compiled genealogies
☐ genealogical periodicals
☐ local and county histories
☐ record abstracts and transcriptions

VITAL RECORDS
☐ amended birth certificates
☐ birth certificates
☐ delayed birth certificates
☐ death certificates
☐ marriage licenses and certificates
☐ stillbirth certificates
☐ divorce/annulment decrees

Source Citation Step-by-Step

 GATHER SOURCE DETAILS.

Collect this information about the source:

- **WHO**: author or agency that created the record, or the provenance of artifacts that are privately owned
- **WHAT**: title, volume, page, or document number
- **WHEN**: date created or published, date you accessed online records
- **WHERE**: publisher and city, microfilm number, URL of online records; for unpublished records, the archive/library or owner's name with city and state

 FORMAT THE CITATION.

Use the sample citations to document your sources in a standard format. Note that not every example will apply perfectly to the particular record you've found. Your goal is to communicate everything a researcher (whether you or someone else) would need to find the source again.

STEP 3 LINK THE SOURCE WITH ITS CITATION.

Record citations and link each fact about your ancestors to the source(s) it came from in one or more of these ways:

- Create a master list of numbered source citations. Add numbers to each ancestor and fact on your charts.
- Use the source citation feature of your genealogy software or online tree. Add a source to every life event and/or individual it documents.
- Write your citations on record copies in the margin or on the back (avoid ink that will bleed through).
- Add citations to digitized documents using a photo-editing program (for a JPG), or the Typewriter tool in the free Adobe Reader (for a PDF).

Anatomy of a Source Citation

1. Title of Record
2. Volume and Page Number
3. Certificate Number

4. Name of Records
5. Date of Event
6. Format of Record
7. Author Name

8. Database Name
9. Website URL
10. Date Accessed
11. Notes

EXAMPLE

(1)
Kanawha County, West Virginia, Register of Marriages,

(2)   (3)   (4)
1945, p. 373, #2009, John Thomas Morton—Marie

            (5)   (6)
Rose O'Hotnicky, marr. 24 Nov 1945; digital images,

(7)
West Virginia Division of Culture & History,

(8)   (9)
Vital Research Records Project (http://www.wvculture.org/,

(10)   (11)
accessed 8 January 2012). Note: Groom's surname indexed

as "Morlon."

Citation Resources

The American Genealogist journal
<americangenealogist.com>

Board for Certification of Genealogists: Genealogical Proof Standard
<www.bcgcertification.org/ethics-standards>

Evidence Explained: Citing History Sources from Artifacts to Cyberspace
by Elizabeth Shown Mills, third edition revised (Genealogical Publishing
Co., 2017)

FamilySearch Wiki: Cite Your Sources
<familysearch.org/learn/wiki/en Cite_Your_Sources_(Source_Footnotes)>

"How Do I Cite This Record Found on MyHeritage?"
<www.geneamusings.com/2014/05/how-do-i-cite-this-record-i-found-
on.html>

"An Image Citation How-To"
<legalgenealogist.com/blog/2014/03/17/an-image-citation-how-to>

Mastering Genealogical Proof
by Tom Jones (National Genealogical Society, 2013)

National Genealogical Society Quarterly
<www.ngsgenealogy.org/cs/ngsq>

The New England Historical and Genealogical Register
<www.americanancestors.org/browse/publications/the-register>

Source Citation Examples

Record	Citation
Birth, Marriage, and Death Records	
Birth certificate ordered from a state health department	Ohio Department of Health, birth certificate no. 11273 (2 February 1931), William Steele; Division of Vital Statistics, Columbus.
County register of births from state archives website	Mason County, West Virginia, Register of Births, 1868, p. 161, line 260, for "Francisco," child of Ambrose and Susan Roush, b. 26 November 1868; digital images, West Virginia Division of Culture & History, Vital Research Records Project (http://www.wvculture.org/vrr: accessed 11 December 2013).
County marriage license from library's online collection	Florida, Hillsborough County, Marriage Licenses, Thomas S.L. Smith and Catherine McCrea, marr. 21 Jan 1881, digital images (http://digital.lib.usf.edu/SFS0002179/00001/pdf: accessed 4 February 2014), University of South Florida Library, Special Collections, Hillsborough County Marriage Records.
Death certificate found on state archives website	Missouri, "Missouri Death Certificates, 1910–1962," digital images, Missouri Digital Heritage (http://www.sos.mo.gov/archives/resources/deathcertificates: accessed 5 June 2011). No. 22056, Mary Susan Miller, Platte County, 27 April 1920.
Cemetery burials from an online index	Margaret Ivey, compiler. "Hall Cemetery," database, Camden County Missouri Genweb (http://camden.mo-genweb.org/hallcemetery.html: accessed 25 April 2014), database entry for Sarah Morley (1777–1860).
Tombstone you visited	Old St. Joseph Cemetery (Cincinnati, Hamilton County, Ohio), Henry A. Seeger marker, section 4, lot 6, grave 7; personally read, 19 February 2012.
Tombstone photo found online	Findagrave.com, Find A Grave, digital images (http://www.findagrave.com: accessed 12 May 2011), photograph, gravestone for Thomas Selby (1817–1886), Linn Creek, Camden County, Missouri.

Record	Citation
Censuses	
1840 census from FamilySearch.org	1840 U.S. census, Allegany County, Maryland, population schedule, Cumberland, p. 11, line 8. Mathias Rizer; digital image; FamilySearch.org (https://familysearch. org/search/collection/1786457: accessed 25 April, 2014); citing "1840 United States Federal Census" index provided by Ancestry.com, citing NARA microfilm publication M704, roll 156; FHL microfilm 0013182. *Note: Ancestry.com provides the index for the 1790-to-1840 censuses on FamilySearch.org, so citations for these censuses from FamilySearch should credit Ancestry.com for the index, as well as the National Archives microfilm from which Ancestry.com's index is derived. The FHL microfilm number references the images FamilySearch uses.*
1870 census from Ancestry.com	1870 U.S. census, Hamilton County, Ohio, population schedule, Cincinnati 9th Ward, p. 64, dwelling 112, family 565, George and Elisbeth Devenbrock, digital images, Ancestry.com (http://www.ancestry.com: accessed 24 March 2012); citing NARA microfilm publication M593.
Church Records	
Baptismal register from microfilmed church records	St Joseph's Catholic Church Records, 1856-1970, microfilm publication, 3 reels (Frankfort, Kentucky: Kentucky Historical Society, 1992), roll 1, arranged by date, see 8 December 1907, Baptism of Urban Thoss.
City Directories	
City directory entry found on Google Books	Williams Cincinnati Directory, June 1878. (Cincinnati, Ohio: Williams & Co., 1878), p. 714, entry for "Norris, Edward Sr."; digital image, Google Books (http://www. books.google.com: accessed 17 May 2013).
Deeds and Land Records	
Deed from deed book at county courthouse	Lee County, Florida, Deeds, 42:332–333, Isaac B. Smith to Adah Hayes Smith, 14 September 1914; Lee County Clerk of Courts, Fort Myers.
Land patent from BLM/GLO website	Bureau of Land Management, "Land Patent Search," digital images, General Land Office Records (http://www. glorecords.blm.gov: accessed 5 October 2013), entry for Jacob Craft (warrantee) to Eli Owen (grantee), Black Hawk County, Iowa, no. 33367.

Record	Citation
Home Sources	
Loose family Bible pages in a family member's possession	Smith Family Bible Records, 1830-1888, loose family record pages from unknown Bible; privately held by Jill A. Marshall, 321 Main St., Cincinnati, Ohio, 45201; owned since 2003. Original owner unknown. Abraham Smith to Edward J. Smith about 1955, to Francine (Smith) Marshall in 1992, to Jill A. Marshall (great-grandaughter) in 1988.
Letter in a family member's possession	George Rapport (St. Louis, Missouri) to "My darling wife" [Diantha Gray Rapport], letter, 29 December 1863. Privately held by Stephen Noble, Jr., Nashville, Tennessee, 1998. Diantha's papers passed to daughter Emile Handook, thence to her grandson Stephen Noble Sr. and to his son Stephen Noble Jr.
Oral history interview	Anna Bordeaux, mother of Alexander Bordeaux (New Orleans, Louisiana), interview by Alexander Bordeaux, 24 December 1999; digital audio file privately held by interviewer, Atlanta, Georgia, 2012.
Immigration Records	
Online passenger list (index entry only)	"Hamburg Passagierlisten, 1850–1934," database, Ancestry.com (http://ancestry.com : accessed 28 July 2011), entry for Mikal Fenzak, departed 9 November 1883 [no ship stated].
Online passenger list (with images)	Passenger Record Search, 1892–1924, digital images, Statue of Liberty-Ellis Island Foundation (http://ellisisland.org: accessed 14 August 2013), entry for Verona Straka, age 22, arrived 26 July 1922 on the S.S. Orduna; citing National Archives microfilm publication T715, roll 3155, page 77, line 12.
Declaration of Intention to Naturalize found on Fold3 website	"Naturalization Petition and Record Books for the US District Court for the Northern District of Ohio, Eastern Division, Cleveland, 1907-1946," digital images, Fold3.com (http://www.fold3.com/image/171341739: accessed 9 December 2013), declaration no. 77526, Fadlallah Joseph Haddad; citing Naturalization Petition and Record Books for the U.S. District Court for the Northern District of Ohio, Eastern Division, Cleveland, 1907-1946, National Archives microfilm publication M1995, roll 0251.

Record	Citation
Military Records	
Civil War service records found on Fold3	"Civil War Service Records, Union Records, Kentucky" digital images, Fold3 (http://www.fold3.com: accessed 14 May 2014), 53rd Regiment, Co. A, entry for Frank Thoss; citing National Archives microfilm publication Compiled Service Records of Volunteer Union Soldiers Who Served in Organizations From the State of Kentucky, M405, roll 496.
WWI draft card found on Ancestry.com	"U.S., World War I Draft Registration Cards, 1917–1918," digital images, Ancestry.com (http://ancestry.com: accessed 12 September 2011), Summit County, Ohio, Akron City, Draft Board 2, entry for Edward Seeger; citing National Archives microfilm publication World War I Selective Service System Draft Registration Cards, 1917–1918 , M1509.
Newspapers	
News article digitized online	Western Newspaper Union News Service, "Four Persons Killed: Train Hits Auto at Scene of Many Fatalities," *Akron Weekly Pioneer Press*, 12 November 1915, digital images, Colorado Historic Newspapers Collection (http://www.coloradohistoricnewspapers.org : accessed 3 November 2013), p. 1, col. 1.
News obituary from Chronicling America website	"Obituary of Wm. M. Brownlee," *The Abingdon Virginian*, 13 November 1863, p. 3, col. 3; digital images, Chronicling America: Historic American Newspapers, Library of Congress (http://chroniclingamerica.loc.gov : accessed 16 July 2013).
Probate Records	
Estate inventory file found at FamilySearch.org	"Ohio, Hamilton County Records, 1791-1994," digital images, FamilySearch.org (https://familysearch.org/search/collection/2141016 : accessed 31 Mar 2014), probate record for Henry A. Seeger, vol 148, p. 309-310, file no. 94915.

Record	Citation
Published Books	
Published book found on Google Books	Joel Musell's Sons, *History of Schuylkill County, PA with Illustrations and Biographical Sketches of Some of its Prominent Men and Pioneers* (W. W. Munsell & Co: New York, 1881), 282, digital images, Google Books (http://www.books.google.com: accessed 2 August 2012).
Compiled family history from the library	Rachel Maretta Homer Crockett, *Homer Family History* (s. n.: Salt Lake City, Utah, 1942), p. 63.
Social Security Records	
Social Security application (SS-5) ordered from the Social Security Administration	U.S. Social Security Administration, Application for Account Number, Michael Joseph Haddad, no. 286-03-8445.
Social Security Death Index entry found at FamilySearch.org	U.S. Social Security Administration, "United States Social Security Death Index," database, FamilySearch.org (https://familysearch.org/search/collection/1202535: accessed 05 May 2014), entry for Josephine Depenbrock, no. 302-40-8723.

2

US STATE RESEARCH

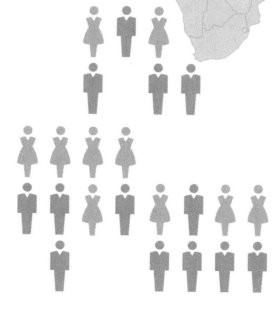

US State Fast Facts

State	Statehood	Public or State Land State	First Extant US Census	Statewide Vital Records Begin		
				Birth	Marriage	Death
AL Alabama	1819	Public	1830	1908	1936	1908
AK Alaska	1959	Public	1900	1913	1913	1913
AZ Arizona	1912	Public	1870	1909	1909	1909
AR Arkansas	1836	Public	1830	1914	1917	1914
CA California	1850	Public	1850	1905	1905	1905
CO Colorado	1876	Public	1860 (as four territories), 1870 (as Colorado Territory), 1880 (as a state)	1907	1907	1907
CT Connecticut	1788	State	1790	1897	1897	1897
DE* Delaware	1787	State	1800	1861	1847	1881
FL Florida	1845	Public	1830	1899	1927	1899
GA Georgia	1788	State	1820	1919	1952	1919
HI Hawaii	1959	State	1900	1842	1842	1859
ID Idaho	1890	Public	1850 (as Oregon Territory)	1911	1947	1911

*Delaware's statewide birth and death records stop in 1863 and resume in 1881.

State	Statehood	Public or State Land State	First Extant US Census	Statewide Vital Records Begin		
				Birth	Marriage	Death
IL Illinois	1818	Public	1820	1916	1962	1916
IN Indiana	1816	Public	1820	1907	1958	1899
IA Iowa	1846	Public	1850	1880	1880	1880
KS Kansas	1861	Public	1860	1911	1913	1911
KY Kentucky	1792	State	1810	1911	1958	1911
LA* Louisiana	1812	Public	1810	1914	none	1914
ME Maine	1820	State	1790	1892	1892	1892
MD Maryland	1788	State	1790	1898	1950	1898
MA Massachusetts	1788	State	1790	1841	1841	1841
MI Michigan	1837	Public	1820	1867	1867	1867
MN Minnesota	1858	Public	1820 (in Michigan Territory)	1900	1958	1908
MS Mississippi	1817	Public	1820	1912	1926	1912
MO Missouri	1821	Public	1830	1910	1881	1910
MT Montana	1889	Public	1870	1907	1943	1907
NE Nebraska	1867	Public	1860	1905	1909	1905
NV Nevada	1864	Public	1850	1911	1968	1911
NH New Hampshire	1788	State	1790	1901	1901	1901

*Louisiana birth records are kept in parish clerk offices.

State	Statehood	Public or State Land State	First Extant US Census	Statewide Vital Records Begin		
				Birth	Marriage	Death
NJ New Jersey	1787	State	1830 (Cumberland County only in 1800)	1848	1848	1848
NM New Mexico	1912	Public	1850	1920	1920	1920
NY New York	1788	State	1790	1880	1880	1880
NC North Carolina	1789	State	1790	1913	1962	1913
ND North Dakota	1889	Public	1900	1907	1925	1907
OH Ohio	1803	Public	1820 (Washington County only in 1810)	1908	1949	1908
OK Oklahoma	1907	Public	1860	1908	1908	1908
OR Oregon	1859	Public	1850	1903	1906	1903
PA Pennsylvania	1787	State	1798	1906	1885	1906
RI Rhode Island	1790	State	1790	1853	1853	1853
SC South Carolina	1788	State	1790	1915	1950	1915
SD South Dakota	1889	Public	1900	1905	1905	1905
TN* Tennessee	1796	State	1830	1908	1945	1908
TX* Texas	1845	State	1850	1903	1966	1903
UT Utah	1896	Public	1850	1905	1887	1905

*Tennessee has no statewide birth or death records for 1913. Texas was established as the Republic of Texas (not a state or territory) in 1836.

State	Statehood	Public or State Land State	First Extant US Census	Statewide Vital Records Begin		
				Birth	Marriage	Death
VT Vermont	1791	State	1790	1955	1955	1955
VA Virginia	1788	State	1810 (partial)	1912	1912	1912
WA Washington	1889	Public	1860	1907	1968	1907
WV West Virginia	1863	State	1870 (earlier censuses as part of Virginia)	1917	1964	1917
WI Wisconsin	1848	Public	1820	1907	1907	1907
WY Wyoming	1890	Public	1870	1909	1941	1909

US State Archives

Alabama Department of Archives and History
<www.archives.state.al.us>

Alaska State Library <library.alaska.gov>

Arizona State Library, Archives and Public Records <azlibrary.gov>

Arkansas History Commission <archives.arkansas.gov>

California State Archives <www.sos.ca.gov/archives>

Colorado State Archives <www.colorado.gov/archives>

Connecticut State Library/State Archives <ctstatelibrary.org/state-archives>

Delaware Public Archives <archives.delaware.gov>

Florida Division of Library and Information Services, State Library and Archives
<dos.myflorida.com/library-archives>

Georgia Archives <www.georgiaarchives.org>

Hawaii State Archives <ags.hawaii.gov/archives>

Idaho State Historical Society <history.idaho.gov>

Illinois State Archives
<www.cyberdriveillinois.com/departments/archives>

Indiana Archives and Records Administration <www.in.gov/iara>

State Historical Society of Iowa <iowaculture.gov/history>

Kansas Historical Society <www.kshs.org>

Kentucky Department for Libraries and Archives <kdla.ky.gov/Pages/default.aspx>

Louisiana State Archives <www.sos.la.gov/HistoricalResources/LearnAboutTheArchives/Pages/default.aspx>

Maine State Archives <www.maine.gov/sos/arc>

Maryland State Archives <msa.maryland.gov>

Massachusetts Archives Division <www.sec.state.ma.us/arc>

Archives of Michigan <www.michigan.gov/archivesofmi>

Minnesota State Archives <www.mnhs.org/preserve/records>

Mississippi Department of Archives and History
<www.mdah.ms.gov>

Missouri State Archives <www.sos.mo.gov/archives>

Montana Historical Society <mhs.mt.gov>

History Nebraska <history.nebraska.gov>

Nevada State Library, Archives & Public Records <nsla.libguides.com/
home>

New Hampshire Division of Archives and Records Management
<sos.nh.gov/Arch_Rec_Mgmt.aspx>

New Jersey State Archives
<www.nj.gov/state/archives/index.html>

New Mexico State Records Center and Archives
<www.nmcpr.state.nm.us/archives/about-the-archives>

New York State Archives Cultural Education Center
<www.archives.nysed.gov>

North Carolina Office of Archives and History
<www.history.ncdcr.gov>

North Dakota State Archives <history.nd.gov/archives>

Ohio Historical Society Archives/Library
<www.ohiohistory.org>

Oklahoma State Archives and Records Management
<libraries.ok.gov/state-government/archives-and-records>

Oregon State Archives <sos.oregon.gov/archives/pages/default.aspx>

Pennsylvania State Archives <www.phmc.pa.gov/Archives/pages/default.aspx>

Puerto Rico General Archive (Archivo General de Puerto Rico) <www.icp.pr.gov>

Rhode Island State Archives <sos.ri.gov/divisions/Civics-And-Education/archives>

South Carolina Department of Archives and History <scdah.sc.gov>

South Dakota State Archives <history.sd.gov/archives>

Tennessee State Library and Archives <sos.tn.gov/tsla>

Texas State Library and Archives Commission <www.tsl.texas.gov>

Utah Division of Archives and Records Service <archives.utah.gov>

Vermont State Archives and Records Administration <www.sec.state.vt.us/archives-records.aspx>

Library of Virginia Records Management <www.lva.virginia.gov/agencies/records>

Washington, DC Archives <www.archives.gov/dc>

Washington State Archives <www.sos.wa.gov/archives>

West Virginia State Archives <www.wvculture.org/history/archives/wvsamenu.html>

Wisconsin Historical Society <www.wisconsinhistory.org>

Wyoming State Archives <wyoarchives.state.wy.us>

Most Populous US Cities Throughout Time

CENSUS YEAR

RANKING	1790	1800	1810	1820	1830	1840
1	New York City	New York City	New York City	New York City	New York City	New York City
2	Philadelphia	Philadelphia	Philadelphia	Philadelphia	Baltimore	Baltimore
3	Boston	Baltimore	Baltimore	Baltimore	Philadelphia	New Orleans
4	Charleston, SC	Boston	Boston	Boston	Boston	Philadelphia
5	Baltimore	Charleston, SC	Charleston, SC	New Orleans	New Orleans	Boston
6	Northern Liberties, PA*	Northern Liberties, PA*	Northern Liberties, PA*	Charleston, SC	Charleston, SC	Cincinnati
7	Salem, MA	Southwark, PA*	New Orleans	Northern Liberties, PA*	Northern Liberties, PA*	Brooklyn, NY**
8	Newport, RI	Salem, MA	Southwark, PA*	Southwark, PA*	Cincinnati	Northern Liberties, PA*
9	Providence, RI	Providence, RI	Salem, MA	Washington	Albany, NY	Albany, NY
10	Marble-head, MA/ Southwark, PA*	Norfolk, VA	Albany, NY	Salem, MA	Southwark, PA*	Charleston, SC

*Northern Liberties and Southwark became part of Philadelphia in 1854.
**Brooklyn became part of a larger, consolidated New York City in 1898.

CENSUS YEAR

RANKING	1850	1860	1870	1880	1890	1900
1	New York City	New York City	New York City	New York City	New York City	New York City
2	Baltimore	Philadelphia	Philadelphia	Philadelphia	Chicago	Chicago
3	Boston	Brooklyn, NY**	Brooklyn, NY**	Brooklyn, NY**	Philadelphia	Philadelphia
4	Philadelphia	Baltimore	St. Louis	Chicago	Brooklyn, NY**	St. Louis
5	New Orleans	Boston	Chicago	Boston	St. Louis	Boston
6	Cincinnati	New Orleans	Baltimore	St. Louis	Boston	Baltimore
7	Brooklyn, NY**	Cincinnati	Boston	Baltimore	Baltimore	Cleveland
8	St. Louis	St. Louis	Cincinnati	Cincinnati	San Francisco	Buffalo, NY
9	Spring Garden, PA*	Chicago	New Orleans	San Francisco	Cincinnati	San Francisco
10	Albany, NY	Buffalo, NY	San Francisco	New Orleans	Cleveland	Cincinnati

*Spring Garden became part of Philadelphia in 1854.
**Brooklyn became part of a larger, consolidated New York City in 1898.

CENSUS YEAR

RANKING	1910	1920	1930	1940	1950	1960
1	New York City	New York City	New York City	New York City	New York City	New York City
2	Chicago	Chicago	Chicago	Chicago	Chicago	Chicago
3	Philadelphia	Philadelphia	Philadelphia	Philadelphia	Philadelphia	Los Angeles
4	St. Louis	Detroit	Detroit	Detroit	Los Angeles	Philadelphia
5	Boston	Cleveland	Los Angeles	Los Angeles	Detroit	Detroit
6	Cleveland	St. Louis	Cleveland	Cleveland	Baltimore	Baltimore
7	Baltimore	Boston	St. Louis	Baltimore	Cleveland	Houston
8	Pittsburgh	Baltimore	Baltimore	St. Louis	St. Louis	Pittsburgh
9	Detroit	Pittsburgh	Boston	Boston	Washington, DC	Washington, DC
10	Buffalo, NY	Los Angeles	Pittsburgh	Pittsburgh	Boston	St. Louis

CENSUS YEAR

RANKING	1970	1980	1990	2000	2010	2020 *(est.)*
1	New York City	New York City	New York City	New York City	New York City	*New York City*
2	Chicago	Chicago	Los Angeles	Los Angeles	Los Angeles	*Los Angeles*
3	Los Angeles	Los Angeles	Chicago	Chicago	Chicago	*Chicago*
4	Philadelphia	Philadelphia	Houston	Houston	Houston	*Miami*
5	Detroit	Houston	Philadelphia	Philadelphia	Philadelphia	*Atlanta*
6	Houston	Detroit	San Diego	Phoenix, AZ	Phoenix, AZ	*Philadelphia*
7	Baltimore	Dallas, TX	Detroit	San Diego	San Antonio, TX	*Dallas, TX*
8	Dallas, TX	San Diego	Dallas, TX	Dallas, TX	San Diego	*Houston*
9	Washington, DC	Phoenix, AZ	Phoenix, AZ	San Antonio, TX	Dallas, TX	*Boston*
10	Cleveland	Baltimore	San Antonio, TX	Detroit	San Jose, CA	*Washington, DC*

US States, 1959–2018

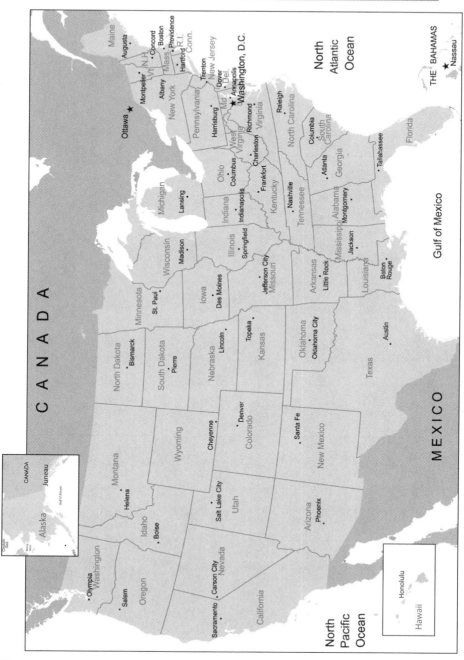

3

LIBRARIES AND ARCHIVES

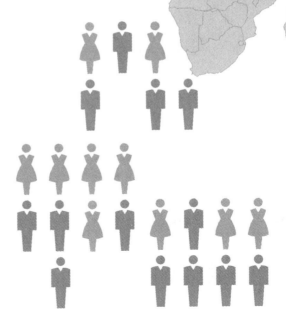

11 Key Genealogy Libraries and Archives

Allen County Public Library (Fort Wayne, Indiana)
<www.acpl.lib.in.us>

Clayton Library Center for Genealogical Research (Houston, Texas)
<www.houstonlibrary.org/location/
clayton-library-center-genealogical-research>

Family History Library (Salt Lake City, Utah)
<www.familysearch.org>
Library also has branches (called Family History Centers) all around the
world <www.familysearch.org/locations/centerlocator>

Denver Public Library (Denver, Colorado)
<history.denverlibrary.org>

Library of Congress (Washington, DC)
<www.loc.gov>

Mid-Continent Public Library (Independence, Missouri)
<www.mymcpl.org/genealogy>

National Archives and Records Administration (Washington, DC)
<www.archives.gov>

National Society Daughters of the American Revolution Library
(Washington, DC)
<www.dar.org>

New England Historic Genealogical Society Research Library
(Boston, Massachusetts)
<www.americanancestors.org>

The New York Public Library (New York City, New York)
<www.nypl.org/locations/divisions/milstein>

Public Library of Cincinnati and Hamilton County (Cincinnati, Ohio)

National Archives and Records Administration Regional Locations

NARA Regional Archives	States/Departments Covered
National Archives in Washington, DC <www.archives.gov/dc>	US Congress, US Supreme Court, federal courts and agencies, pre-WWI service records
National Archives at College Park, Maryland <www.archives.gov/college-park>	Civilian agency text records, WWI army records, WWII navy records, multimedia records (images, motion pictures, videos, etc.)
National Archives at St. Louis <www.archives.gov/st-louis>	military personnel files and folders, Civilian Corps records, draft records
Central Plains Region (Kansas City, MO) <www.archives.gov/kansas-city>	Iowa, Kansas, Minnesota, Missouri, Nebraska, North Dakota, and South Dakota
Great Lakes Region (Chicago) <www.archives.gov/chicago>	Illinois, Indiana, Michigan, Minnesota, Ohio, Wisconsin
Mid-Atlantic Region (Philadelphia) <www.archives.gov/philadelphia>	Delaware, Maryland, Pennsylvania, Virginia, West Virginia
Northeast Region (New York) <www.archives.gov/nyc>	New York, New Jersey, Puerto Rico, US Virgin Islands
Northeast Region (Boston) <www.archives.gov/boston>	Connecticut, Maine, Massachusetts, New Hampshire, Rhode Island, Vermont
Pacific Alaska Region (Seattle) <www.archives.gov/seattle>	Alaska, Idaho, Oregon, Washington
Pacific Region (Riverside, CA) <www.archives.gov/riverside>	Arizona, southern California, Nevada (Clark County only)
Pacific Region (San Francisco) <www.archives.gov/san-francisco>	American Samoa, northern and central California, Guam, Hawaii, Nevada (except for Clark County)
Rocky Mountain Region (Denver, CO) <www.archives.gov/denver>	Colorado, Montana, New Mexico, North Dakota, South Dakota, Utah, Wyoming
Southeast Region (Atlanta) <www.archives.gov/atlanta>	Alabama, Florida, Georgia, Kentucky, Mississippi, North Carolina, South Carolina, Tennessee
Southwest Region (Fort Worth, TX) <www.archives.gov/fort-worth>	Arkansas, Louisiana, Oklahoma, Texas

6 Tips for Requesting Genealogy Records

1. Before you send a request, search the library's or archive's website to verify that it has the materials you need. If you can't find the information, e-mail or call the reference or genealogy desk and ask.

2. Look online for the library's instructions for requesting records. Follow them exactly, providing the information the library asks for about the ancestor who's the subject of the record, using the format specified (such as e-mail or a typed letter) and including any fees.

3. Double-check the name spellings and dates in your request to eliminate typos (which can make the record impossible for a librarian to find). Include any nicknames or maiden names the ancestor may appear with.

4. Be realistic: Don't ask a librarian to search several years' worth of records, or to hand you a completed pedigree chart. If the scope of your request goes beyond the time a librarian can devote to it, he or she may recommend you hire a private researcher.

5. If you don't receive a response within a couple of months, send a polite follow-up with a copy of your first request for reference.

6. As an alternative to requesting a record from a distant library, you may be able to borrow it through interlibrary loan. Ask for assistance at your local library's reference or genealogy desk.

Sample Record Request Letter

Dear Sir or Madam:

I would like to order a copy of the marriage document for my grandparents, Michael John Mullinger and Jean Louise "Lou" Miller, who were married in Cincinnati, Hamilton County, Ohio, on Oct. 30, 1918. Michael was 23 at the time and Jean was 20.

Please also look under Mallinger, a common misspelling for Michael's surname.

As directed on your website, I have enclosed a check for the amount of $23.

Please mail the document to me at my mailing address, 123 Main St., Anywhere, USA, 12345. If you have any questions, you may contact me at (123) 456-7890 or via e-mail at jrdoe@hotmail.com.

Thank you very much for your assistance in this matter.

Sincerely,
John R. Doe

Online Digitized Family Histories

$ = subscription required to access most records

$ Ancestry.com Family and Local Histories <www.ancestry.com>

Family History Books <books.familysearch.org>

Google Books <books.google.com>

HeritageQuest Online Family and Local Histories
<heritagequestonline.com> (available through subscribing libraries)

Internet Archive <www.archive.org/details/texts>

Making of America
<collections.library.cornell.edu/moa_new> and
<quod.lib.umich.edu/m/moagrp>

MyHeritage Compilation of Published Sources <www.myheritage.com/
research/collection-90100/compilation-of-published-sources>

$ World Vital Records <www.worldvitalrecords.com>

4

NAMES

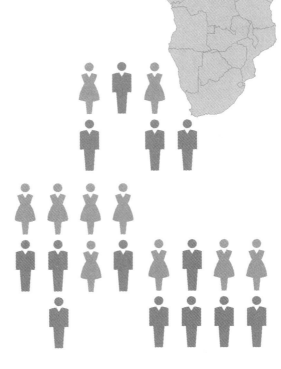

Types of Surnames

PATRONYMIC

The patronymic system bases a child's surname on the father's given name. This type of name is found throughout the world, but is especially common in Ireland, the Scottish highlands, Wales, Spain, and Scandinavia. Various cultures have different prefixes and suffixes that may indicate a patronymic name. Those include:

- **Armenian**: *-yan*, *-ian* as in Hovnanian
- **Danish**: *-sen* as in Sorensen
- **Dutch**: *-zoon, -sz, -dochter, -dr*
- **English**: *-son, Fitz-, -s* as in Edwards; *-ing* as in Browning ("son of Brun")
- **Greek**: *-opoulos* as in Theodoropoulos ("son of Theodore")
- **Hebrew**: *ben* as in Ben-Yehuda
- **Irish**: *O'* as in O'Hara ("grandson of Eaghra")
- **Italian**: *De-, Di-* as in DeCarlo
- **Norwegian**: *-sen, -datter*
- **Portuguese**: *-az, -es* as in Gomes ("son of Gomo")
- **Romanian**: *-escu* as in Tadescu
- **Russian**: *-ovna, -ovich* as in Pavlovich
- **Polish**: *-wicz* as in Danielewicz
- **Scottish**: *-son, Fitz-, Mac, Mc* as in McCall ("son of Cachal")
- **Spanish**: *-es, -ez* as in Alvarez ("son of Alva")
- **Swedish**: *-dotter; -son* as in Olafson ("son of Olaf")
- **Turkish**: *-oglu* as in Turnacioglu
- **Ukrainian**: *-ovich, -ovna, -enko* as in Kovalenko
- **Welsh**: *-ap, -ab, p-* as in Upjohn ("son of John"), *b-* as in Bowen ("son of Owen")

PLACE-BASED

This type of name is derived from a nearby geographical or natural feature such as a hill, brook, valley, bridge; a place of origin; or ownership of a manor or village. Place-based names are common in England, Germany, and France. Examples include:

- **Chinese**: Li ("plum tree"), Wong ("field," "wide sea" or "ocean")
- **Dutch**: Roosevelt ("rose field"), Van Pelt ("from Pelt")
- **English**: names with suffixes -*ton*, -*wick*, *ley*, -*thorpe*, -*ham*, -*land* and -*ford;* England, Englander, Engel, Engelman (from England)
- **French**: Cassell ("chateau" or "castle"), De Long ("from the large place")
- **German**: Steinbach ("stony brook"); names with -*er* added to a locality, as in Berliner ("from Berlin"); Allemand (from Germany)
- **Italian**: Lombard, Lombardi, Lombardo ("from Lombardy"), Napoli ("from Naples")
- **Polish**: Bielski ("from Bielsk"), Wisniewski ("from Wiznia")
- **Portuguese**: Ferreira ("from Ferreira," meaning "iron mine" or "workshop"), Teixeira ("place of yew trees")
- **Spanish**: Cortez ("court" or "town"), Morales ("mulberry tree"), Navarro ("the plain among hills")

OCCUPATIONAL

This type of name is derived from an occupation, such as Smith, Miller, Taylor and Clark. Occupational surnames are among the most common surnames in the United States.

NICKNAME-BASED

These names describe personal appearance (stature, hair, eyes, complexion), characteristics (strong, bold, brave), financial status, habits, or skills. They may be combined with patronymics; for example, the Italian D'Onofrio ("son of a giant"). Nickname-based names are common in Italy and Portugal. For example, names that mean "poor" are Powers or Poor (English), Scholl (German), or Chudak (Czech or Slovak).

Cultural Naming Traditions

DUTCH

Many surnames or middle names were patronymic until 1811, when permanent surnames were required.

FRENCH

Multiple Christian names; nicknames may be used instead of given names.

GERMAN

First name may be a "prefix name" given at baptism; the middle name was the *Rufnahmen* ("call name") the individual used. For example, Johann Christian Miller may have been known as Christian Miller.

GREEK

First son named after paternal grandfather, first daughter named after paternal grandmother, second son named after maternal grandfather, and so on. For middle initials, children took the first letter of the father's given name. Married women changed the middle initial to the first letter of the husband's name.

HUNGARIAN

Family name commonly goes before the given name. Women often add the suffix -*né* to the husband's name; for example, Erzébet might be in records as Kovács Mátyásné (Mrs. Mátyás Kovács, or Matthew's wife).

IRISH

Given names tend to repeat over generations.

ITALIAN

First son named after paternal grandfather; first daughter, after paternal grandmother; second son, after maternal grandfather; second daughter, after maternal grandmother. Third son and daughter named after the parents. Children may be named after deceased siblings (necronymics).

JEWISH

Ashkenazi generally name children after deceased relatives. Sephardim often name children after living grandparents, with first son after the paternal grandfather, first daughter after maternal grandmother, and so on.

POLISH

Catholics often named a child after a saint whose feast day was on or near the birth or baptism.

PORTUGUESE, SPANISH

Prefixes such as *de la* were often added to surnames. Married women typically kept their maiden names. Children took both the father's and mother's last names, using the father's surname as the family name. For example, when Julia Jimenez Montero marries Alejandro Ignacio Perez, she remains Julia Jimenez Montero, possibly adding her husband's family name to become Julia Jimenez Montero de Perez. In Spain, their daughter, Marta, would become Marta Perez Jimenez. In Portugal, where the second surname is the man's family name, she would be Marta Jimenez Perez.

SCANDINAVIAN

Patronymic surnames are common; permanent surnames became official in 1901 in Sweden and 1923 in Norway. Norwegians also often used a second last name based on their farm: Olav Petersen Dal became Olav Petersen Li after moving to the Li farm. Men may have taken different surnames while in the military, and may have changed them back later.

SCOTTISH

The first son was named after the paternal grandfather; second son, after the maternal grandfather; third son, after the father; fourth son, after the father's brother; first daughter, after the paternal grandmother; second daughter, after the maternal grandmother; third daughter, after the mother; fourth daughter, after the mother's sister.

15 Most Common
US Surnames, 1850

1. Smith	**6.** Davis	**11.** Thompson
2. Brown	**7.** Williams	**12.** White
3. Miller	**8.** Wilson	**13.** Moore
4. Johnson	**9.** Clark	**14.** Martin
5. Jones	**10.** Taylor	**15.** Baker

15 Most Common
US Surnames, 2010

1. Smith	**6.** Garcia	**11.** Hernandez
2. Johnson	**7.** Miller	**12.** Lopez
3. Williams	**8.** Davis	**13.** Gonzalez
4. Brown	**9.** Rodriguez	**14.** Wilson
5. Jones	**10.** Martinez	**15.** Anderson

Tips for Researching
Common Surnames

1. Learn as much identifying information about the ancestor as possible, such as where he lived and his birth year and place, to rule out others with the same name.

2. Anchor the person with a spouse, child, or other person who has an uncommon name.

3. Make a chronology of the person's life events to compare with records of same-named individuals.

Nicknames and Variations
for Popular Names

FEMALE

Abigail: Abby, Gail, Nabby

Barbara: Babs, Barb, Barbie, Bobbie, Bonnie

Carolyn/Caroline: Caddie, Callie, Carol, Carrie, Lena, Lynn

Catherine: Cathryn, Cathy, Katharine, Kathleen, Karen, Katie, Kay, Kit, Kittie, Rhynie, Rina, Trina

Christine/Christina: Chris, Christiana, Crissy, Christy, Ina, Kissy, Kit, Kris, Krissy, Kristina, Kristine, Tina, Xina

Elaine/Eleanor: Elena, Ella, Ellen, Ellie, Elsie, Helen, Lana, Lainie, Lena, Leonora, Nell, Nellie, Nora

Elizabeth: Bess, Bessie, Bet, Beth, Betsy, Betty, Bitsy, Eli, Eliza, Elsie, Ibby, Libby, Lisa, Lish, Liz, Liza, Lizbet, Lizzie, Tess

Margaret: Margareta, Magdelene, Daisy, Greta, Madge, Maggie, Marge, Margie, Margo, Meg, Midge, Peg, Peggy

Mary/Maria: Mae, Mamie, May, Mattie, Mimi, Molly, Polly

Melissa: Lisa, Lissa, Mel, Missy

Sarah: Sally

Susan/Susanna: Anna, Hannah, Nan, Nanny, Sue, Sukey, Susie, Suzanne, Suze

Theresa: Terrie, Tess, Tessie, Tessa, Thursa, Tracy

MALE

Alexander: Al, Alastair, Alex, Alisdair, Alistair, Eleck, Sandy, Zan

Andrew: Andy, Drew

Benjamin: Ben, Bennie, Benjy, Jamie

Charles: Carl, Charlie, Charley, Chick, Chuck

Edward/Edmund: Ed, Eddie, Eddy, Ned, Ted, Teddy

Frederick/Alfred: Al, Fred, Freddie, Freddy, Fritz, Rick

James/Jameson: Jamie, Jem, Jim, Jimi, Jimmy, Mamey

Jonathan: Eon, Ian, Jack, Jock, John, Johannes, Johnny, Jon, Nathan

Lawrence/Laurence: Larry, Lon, Lonny, Lorne, Lorry

Matthew/Matthias: Matt, Matty, Thias, Thys

Michael: Micah, Mick, Mickey, Mickie, Micky, Mike

Patrick: Paddy, Pat, Pate

Richard: Dick, Dickie, Dickson, Rich, Rick, Ricky

Robert: Bob, Bobby, Dob, Dobbin, Rob, Robbie, Robin, Robby, Rupert

Thomas: Tam, Tom, Thom, Tomi, Tommie, Tommy

William: Bill, Billy, Will, Willy

Zachariah/Zachary: Zach, Zachy, Zack, Zak, Zeke

Name Translations

English	German/Dutch	Latin
Andrew	Andreas	Andreas
Catherine	Kat(h)arina	Catherina/Ecaterina
Charles	Carl/Karl	Carolus
Edward	Eduard	Eduardus
Elizabeth	Elisabeth	Elisabetha
George	Georg, Jürgen	Georgius
James/Jacob	Jakob	Iacobus, Iacomus
Jane	Johanna	Ioanna
John	Johann/Hans	Ioannes/Ionathan
Joseph	Josef	Iosephus
Lawrence	Lorenz, Laurenz, Laürnt	Laurentius
Lewis/Louis	Ludwig	Ludovicus, Aloysius
Margaret	Margareta	Margarita
Matthew	Matthäus	Matthaeus
Mary	Maria/Marie	Maria
Michael	Michael/Michel	Michael
Michelle	Michaela	Michaela
Nicholas	Nikolaus, Nicklaus	Nicolaus
William	Vilhelm/Wilhelm	Gulielmus

French	Polish	Norwegian
André	Andrzej, Jędrzej	Anders, Andreas
Catherine	Katarzyna	Caterina, Kat(h)arina
Charles	Karol	Carl/Karl
Édouard	Edward, Edek, Edzio	Edvard
Élisabeth	Elżbieta, Izabela	Elisabet, Isabel
Georges	Jerzy, Jurek	Georg, Gøran/Jørn, Jørg(en)
Jacques, Jacob	Jakub, Kuba	Jacob/Jakob
Jeanne	Joanna, Janina	Joana, Johanna, Janne
Jean	Jan, Janek, Janusz	Hans, Ivan, Jan, Johan(n)
Joseph	Józef	Josef
Laurent	Laurencjusz, Laurenty, Wawrzyniec	Lars, Laurits/Lauritz, Lorens
Louis	Ludwik, Alojzy	Ludvig
Marguerite/Margot	Małgorzata, Małgosia	Margareta, Marit, Margit
Matthieu	Maciej, Mateusz	Mathias, Matteus
Marie	Maria, Marzena	Maria, Maiken
Michel	Michał	Mikael, Mikkel
Michèle	Michalina	Mikaela
Nicolas	Mikołaj	Niklas, Nils
Guillaume	Wilhelm	Vilhelm

5

GENEALOGY WEBSITES

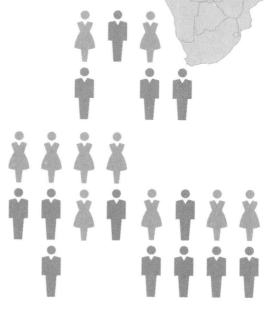

Top Genealogy Websites

$ = subscription required to access most records

AccessGenealogy <www.accessgenealogy.com>
Millions of records from most US states

Afrigeneas <www.afrigeneas.com>
Free slave records, a surnames database, death and marriage databases, and census schedules

$ American Ancestors <www.americanancestors.org>
More than 2,400 databases encompassing 110 million names, including vital records, early American newspapers, court records, military records, Sanborn fire-insurance maps, research journal indexes, and more

$ Ancestry.com <www.ancestry.com>
US census records; many Canadian, England and Wales censuses; US passenger arrivals; military records; vital-records indexes from various US states, Canada, and the United Kingdom; family and local history books; city directories; yearbooks; newspapers; user-contributed family trees (note that most Ancestry.com content is available free at libraries that subscribe to Ancestry Library Edition)

$ Archives.com <www.archives.com>
US census indexes; US and Canadian vital records indexes, passenger indexes, military records indexes, living person search, family tree builder

Bureau of Land Management General Land Office Records
<glorecords.blm.gov/default.aspx>
More than 3 million federal land title records spanning 1820 to 1908, plus Colorado, Idaho, Montana, South Dakota, and North Dakota Master Title Plats, surveyors' field notes, bounty land warrants issued, and more

BYU Idaho
<libguides.byui.edu/familyhistory>
Index of more than 912,000 records from Arizona, Idaho, Nevada, California, western Colorado, Montana, Oregon, Utah, eastern Washington, and Wyoming

Castle Garden <www.castlegarden.org>
Names and basic details for 11 million New York immigrants arriving between 1820 and 1892, as well as some later passengers

Civil War Soldiers & Sailors System
<www.nps.gov/civilwar/soldiers-and-sailors-database.htm>
6.3 million names of Union and Confederate soldiers from 44 states and territories, regimental histories, and battle histories

Cyndi's List <www.cyndislist.com>
Links to more than 275,000 genealogy websites in 180-plus categories

Daughters of the American Revolution <www.dar.org>
Searchable databases including the DAR Genealogical Research System, which contains information on ancestors submitted in member applications

FamilySearch.org <www.familysearch.org>
1850 through 1880, 1900, 1920, 1930 US census records or indexes; US vital records indexes; the Social Security Death Index, 1851, 1871, 1881; 1891 Canadian census indexes; 1881 British Isles census indexes; Mexico 1930 census; Mexican marriages and church records; civil registrations and church records from around the world; 25,000-plus digitized publications

Find A Grave <www.findagrave.com>
More than 170 million grave records, many accompanied by photos

$ Findmypast <www.findmypast.com>
British birth, marriage, and death records; 1841 to 1911 English and Welsh censuses; military records; outbound passenger lists; living person search; family tree building

$ Fold3 <www.fold3.com>
US military records, photos and stories for Revolutionary War, War of 1812, Indian wars, Mexican War, Civil War, World War I, World War II, Korean War, Vietnam War; 1860 and 1930 census; city directories; homestead records; naturalization records

$ GenealogyBank <www.genealogybank.com>
Historical newspapers and books; 130 million obituaries dating back to 1977; the Social Security Death Index; historical documents including military casualty lists, the US Congressional Serial Set and American State Papers

HeritageQuestOnline <www.heritagequestonline.com>
(available through subscribing libraries)
US censuses from 1790 to 1930 (some lack indexes); the Periodical Source Index; Revolutionary War pension and bounty land warrant applications; Freedman's Bank records; the US Serial Set

Immigrant Ships Transcribers Guild <www.immigrantships.net>
Volunteer-submitted transcriptions of more than 11,000 passenger records

JewishGen <www.jewishgen.org>
Family Finder surname database, ShtetlSeeker, Holocaust Database, Worldwide Burial Registry, Yizkor Book Project Database, and more

Library and Archives Canada
<www.bac-lac.gc.ca/eng/discover/genealogy/Pages/introduction.aspx>
Research guides to Canadian records; census records; indexes for passenger records, immigration, military, and land records; photos and more

Library of Congress <www.loc.gov>
The American Memory collection, digitized records and images, American Slave Narratives, National Union Catalog of Manuscript Collections, Chronicling America historical newspaper collection

$ MyHeritage <www.myheritage.com>
Subscription service boasting 94 million records, with special focus on European ancestry; UK, US, Irish, Canadian, and Scandinavian census records; English, Mexican, and German vital records; newspapers; city directories; two billion user-submitted family tree profiles; DNA results

National Archives and Records Administration <www.archives.gov>
Research guides; Access to Archival Databases collection with more than 85 million listings in indexes to military, passenger lists, and other records; the Archival Research Catalog with indexes to 6 million-plus records (includes 153,000 digitized documents or photos)

Nationwide Gravesite Locator <gravelocator.cem.va.gov>
US burials of veterans and their families in VA National Cemeteries; state veterans cemeteries; various other military and Department of Interior cemeteries, as well as some private cemeteries

Newspaper Abstracts <www.newspaperabstracts.com>
69,000-plus pages of abstracts and extracts from historical newspapers, focusing on obituaries, births, marriages, deaths, court notices, land sales, and tax notices

OliveTreeGenealogy <www.olivetreegenealogy.com>
1,500 free ship-list transcriptions and links to off-site passenger lists

$ Onegreatfamily <www.onegreatfamily.com>
More than 190 million searchable names in members' family trees

One-Step Webpages <www.stevemorse.org>
Enhanced searching of databases at Ellis Island, Castle Garden, Ancestry.com, and more; enumeration district finders; and other tools

RootsWeb <rootsweb.ancestry.com>
Records transcriptions, the WorldConnect pedigree file, a surname database, 161,000 message boards, and nearly 30,000 mailing lists

Statue of Liberty & Ellis Island <www.libertyellisfoundation.org>
22 million records of passenger arrivals through the port of New York from 1892 to 1924

TheShipsList <www.theshipslist.com>
Passenger lists, immigration reports, newspaper records, shipwreck information, ship pictures and descriptions, and more

USGenWeb <www.usgenweb.org>
Umbrella site for volunteer-run state and county pages, as well as several special projects; records include transcriptions of censuses, tombstone inscriptions, church records, and more

$ World Vital Records <www.worldvitalrecords.com>
More than 1.2 billion genealogy records, including digitized books; abstracts and transcriptions from books; digitized newspapers; pedigree charts and family group sheets; censuses of England and Wales; and more

Ancestry.com Tips

⭐ **Experiment with different search terms and filters** for the records you want. Keep track of options you try so you don't miss a promising search option or waste time repeating the same searches.

⭐ **Read Ancestry's information page about a collection.** Scroll down on the individual database search page to find coverage details. You might find out the records start after your ancestor died or that records are missing for the place he lived.

⭐ **Use Exact carefully**. You don't want to accidentally exclude relevant records from your search. If the death date is marked Exact, for example, your results will contain only records that have a death date—and most of your ancestor's records were created while he was still alive.

⭐ **Search married and maiden names**.

⭐ **Look for family members** who might also be in the record if you can't find your ancestor.

⭐ **Browse records** if you can't find the right document. Go to the collection search page and click the Browse This Collection link. You'll be able to choose a place, time frame, first letter of the surname, or other browsing option (depending how the original records are organized). Then you can use the back and next arrows to "page" through the records, similarly to how you'd scroll microfilm or flip through a book.

⭐ **View related records**. When you find a record matching your ancestor, look at the Suggested Records sidebar for related records that may name the same person. Check these suggestions carefully, as they may be for people who aren't actually your family.

⭐ **Check the site's message boards <www.ancestry.com/boards>** for the surnames you're researching and the places (typically by county) your family has lived. If you post, use a subject line such as *Harrison family in Ripley County, Ind.* to quickly tell other researchers whether your post might pertain to their families.

⭐ **Consult other users' trees**. Ancestry Member Trees aren't independently verified, so use information from trees only as clues. Don't add data from other trees to yours until you've confirmed the information matches your ancestor and the details are correct. If you're an Ancestry.com subscriber, you can contact the tree's owner to compare notes.

⭐ **Check back for new and updated records**. Ancestry.com regularly adds new databases and updates existing ones, so revisit your searches periodically. Ancestry.com has compiled a list of recently added and updated collections to help you identify new offerings <www.ancestry.com/cs/recent-collections>.

⭐ **Use search wildcards**. Using wildcard characters can help you account for spelling variants and indexing errors. Use a *?* to substitute for one letter in a name, and an * to stand for zero or more letters. For example, a search for *Johns?n* will return records naming Johnsen and Johnson. You can use a wildcard as the first or last letter of a name, but not both: *Han** and **son* are okay, but not **anso**. Names must contain at least three non-wildcard characters.

Shortcut	Purpose
n	Launches a new search by opening a new search form
r	Refines your search (Note: It will launch a search form that's pre-populated using the data you just searched; it also enables you to edit information in a search form without using the back keys or the Edit link.)
p	Previews current record in search result
>	Highlights next record
<	Highlights previous record

FamilySearch.org Tips

⭐ **Browse records**. If you're striking out when keyword-searching for an ancestor's record, consider paging through images of the record instead. FamilySearch.org makes this easy by letting you to jump to a specific page.

⭐ **Set up notifications for family tree profiles**. Anyone can edit your FamilySearch family tree, so FamilySearch.org allows you to receive notifications when someone adds or edits details to an individual's profile. Click the star next to Watch when viewing a profile, and the site will notify you when someone makes changes or adds records.

⭐ **Dive into the FamilySearch Wiki**. The FamilySearch Wiki **<www. familysearch.org/wiki/en/Main_Page>** boasts more than 80,000 free articles about thousands of research topics, from New York City vital records to German gazetteers. These can serve as great introductions to every genealogical topic under the sun and link you to relevant FamilySearch.org collections.

⭐ **Use wildcard characters in searches**. By using wildcard characters, you can broaden your search to include spelling variations—critical when researching records that may have been poorly indexed or mistranscribed. Use a question mark (?) to represent one missing letter, and an asterisk (*) to represent zero or more characters. For example, a search *Henders?n* will return Henderson, Hendersyn, Hendersan, and Hendersen. Likewise, *Han** could return Hanson or Hansen.

⭐ **Switch browsers**. Having trouble viewing records? Try looking at them in a different browser. Some browsers play nicer with FamilySearch.org than others. Copy and paste the URL into a different browser window (such as Google Chrome, Firefox, or Internet Explorer).

⭐ **Keep track of your searches**. If FamilySearch.org hasn't recently updated a collection you're researching, you'll want to avoid repeating your searches. To make the most of your time, keep a log of your searches—what collection(s) you searched, what terms and filters you used, and what results you found (if any). This will keep you from doing the same work over again, plus help you better plan your search strategy.

⭐ **Look for multiple kinds of records**. FamilySearch.org's database holds all kinds of genealogy records, from tax records to probates to passenger lists. From the main search form, you can filter your search by record type. Also remember to browse for records collections by location, so you can see what FamilySearch.org has in your area.

⭐ **Scour premade genealogies**. In addition to records, FamilySearch.org also houses published ancestries, created and submitted by users. Genealogies include the Ancestral File (40 million profiles submitted by users before 2003) and the International Genealogical Index (curated by members of the Church of Jesus Christ of Latter-day Saints). Visit the Genealogies landing page, and enter your search terms to get started. As the site warns, the accuracy of these trees varies, so be sure to back up any data you find here with sources from your own research.

⭐ **Broaden your location search**. Records weren't necessarily kept in the same town in which they were created. Study history, then identify where the records you're looking for are currently held, as this might affect where FamilySearch.org categorizes them. For example, Austrian archives might hold records from some parts of modern Romania, as Austria-Hungary controlled western Romania until World War I. Check the FamilySearch Wiki to determine what locations might have the records you're seeking.

⭐ **Visit a Family History Center**. Check with your local Family history Center **<www.familysearch.org/locations>** to see what offline resources they hold. These repositories, scattered throughout the world, often hold valuable records in book, microfilm, and microfiche formats. Staff members at the facility will also be happy to help you look for researchers, and may know key information about local history and record sets.

Boolean Search Terms

Use these key Boolean "operators" to narrow your online search engine results and eliminate unwanted matches. Remember that capitalization doesn't matter in almost all online searches.

and: Specifies that the term following it must appear in each search result: a search on *Selby and Massachusetts* returns only pages with the words Selby and Massachusetts.

OR: Searches for either of two terms, as in *Dupree OR Dupray OR Dupre OR Dupreen genealogy* (the OR operator must be capitalized in Google searches). The pipe symbol does the same thing: *Dupree | Dupray | Dupre | Dupreen genealogy.*

near: Finds web pages in which two words appear near each other: *"john henry" near "Connecticut."* Neither Google nor Yahoo recognizes this operator.

quotation marks (""): Use to specify that the search term must appear as an exact phrase in every search result. For example, a search on *"Robert Selby"* returns pages with the words Robert and Selby side by side in that order.

minus sign (-): Specifies that the term following it must not appear in search results. For example, search on *Reese -peanut* to find pages with the word Reese but not peanut (useful for eliminating candy results from your Reese surname search).

Google Search Hacks

SEARCH SYNTAXES

- **Site**: To search for content on a specific website, just include *site:* plus the domain name, as in *harriet railey site:rootsweb.ancestry.com*. Use this to focus on particular types of sites, as in *site:.gov* or *site:.org*.

- **URL**: Don't know the exact domain of the site you want to search? Try *inurl:* to find pages on sites with the word genealogy in their address: *railey inurl:genealogy*.

- **Title**: Sites usually put their names in the title bar that appears at the top of your browser, so use Google's intitle: syntax to find "Smithers Family Genealogy" or "Barb's Smithers Home Page." Just type *intitle:smithers genealogy*.

SEARCH TOOLS

- **Dictionary**: Wondering what it means if your ancestor died intestate? Type *define:intestate* to learn he didn't leave a will.

- **Calculator**: Enter an equation into the search box, using * to multiply and / to divide. If your great-grandfather's property was 450x160 feet, input *450*160=* to get the square footage of 72,000.

- **Unit conversion**: This works for various height, weight, and mass measurements. Enter *72000 sq ft* in acres to learn Great-grandpa owned 1.6 acres of land.

- **Currency conversion**: How much will that record request from the British National Archives end up costing you? Just model your search query after the following (substituting the appropriate fee amount in pounds): *10 british pounds in us dollars*. You can even abbreviate this as *10 gpb in usd*. You'll find out the fee's equivalent in dollars.

- **Area codes**: You've located a phone number for someone who may be your distant cousin, but you aren't sure where she lives. Enter *area code 240* to discover she resides in western Maryland.

Google Quick Links

Alerts	<google.com/alerts>
Book Search	<books.google.com>
Calendar	<google.com/calendar>
Cloud Print	<google.com/cloudprint>
Drive	<drive.google.com>
Earth	<earth.google.com>
Gmail	<mail.google.com>
Google+	<plus.google.com>
Image Search	<images.google.com>
Maps	<maps.google.com>
Photos	<photos.google.com>
Toolbar	<toolbar.google.com>
Translate	<translate.google.com>

Genealogy Websites

Account Information Worksheet

Use this worksheet to record your account name and password for genealogy websites like Ancestry.com and FamilySearch.org.

WEBSITE_____

USERNAME/E-MAIL_____

PASSWORD_____

NOTES_____

_____

WEBSITE_____

USERNAME/E-MAIL_____

PASSWORD_____

NOTES_____

_____

WEBSITE_____

USERNAME/E-MAIL_____

PASSWORD_____

NOTES_____

_____

WEBSITE_____

USERNAME/E-MAIL_____

PASSWORD_____

NOTES_____

_____

WEBSITE_____

USERNAME/E-MAIL_____

PASSWORD_____

NOTES_____

_____

WEBSITE_____

USERNAME/E-MAIL_____

PASSWORD_____

NOTES_____

_____

6

COMPUTING

Keyboard Shortcuts

Function	PC	Mac
Open a file	Control-O	Command-O
Close a file	Control-W	Command-W
Quit a program	Control-Q	Command-Q
Create a **new file** or folder	Control-N	Command-N
Save	Control-S	Command-S
Print	Control-P	Command-P
Find	Control-F	Command-F
Select all the data in a document	Control-A	Command-A
Copy selected text	Control-C	Command-C
Cut selected text	Control-X	Command-X
Paste copied or cut text	Control-V	Command-V
Boldface selected text	Control-B	Command-B
Italicize selected text	Control-I	Command-I
Change selected text to **upper- or lowercase**	Shift-F3	Shift-F3
Increase size of selected text	Control-Shift->	Command-Shift->
Decrease size of selected text	Control-Shift-<	Command-Shift-<
Undo	Control-Z	Command-Z

File Format Guide

We've all received a file we didn't know how to open. The secret to identifying a compatible software program lies in the three- or four-letter extension at the end of the file name. This glossary will help you unscramble those mystery letters and identify the format for the file you've received.

AVI: Audio Video Interleave. Most often played on Apple QuickTime or Windows Media Player, this format for sound and video clips is becoming obsolete.

BMP: Windows bitmap. These image files tend to be large because they are uncompressed; they have wide acceptance on Windows systems.

DOC or **DOCX**: If you use Microsoft Word to type genealogy notes or correspondence, the resulting files are DOC or DOCXs. Someone with an older version of Microsoft Word will need to download a file converter or use an online utility to read a DOCX file.

FDB: The native file format for Legacy Family Tree genealogy software.

FTW: The native file format for Family Tree Maker genealogy software.

GED: GEDCOM (short for Genealogical Data Communications). When genealogists who use different family tree programs want to share their family files, they can convert their data to this standard file format that any genealogy software can open.

GIF: Graphics Interchange Format. Most image-editing software, such as Adobe Photoshop Elements or PaintShop Pro, can open this graphics format for still and animated images. Excellent for simple images that contain text, it's most often used for web graphics with a small number of colors (not photos).

HTML: Hypertext Markup Language. This is the predominant programming language for web pages. Open an HTML file in Internet Explorer or another web browser to view the "finished" page; use an HTML or plain-text editor such as Notepad to see or change the coding.

JPG or **JPEG**: Short for Joint Photographic Experts Group, JPG (or JPEG) has become the most widely used format for static photographic images because it can display millions of colors. Any image-editing software can read a JPG.

MOV: Apple Quicktime Movie. MOV is probably the most common multimedia format for saving video or movie files. It's compatible with both Macintosh and Windows platforms.

MP3: One of the most popular audio formats, MP3 compresses sound clips into small files without losing quality. You can play MP3s on a portable device such as an iPhone, or software such as iTunes and Real Player.

MP4: Not to be confused with MP3, MP4 (Moving Pictures Expert Group 4) is among the most popular video file formats, frequently used for creating movies for the Internet. MP4s are compatible with nearly all video players.

PAF: Data files created by the now-defunct Personal Ancestral File software. Several other genealogy programs, including Family Tree Maker, Legacy, and RootsMagic, can import PAF files directly.

PDF: Portable Document Format. Created to ease document exchanges, PDF lets you use the free Adobe Reader to view a file exactly as it was designed, even without the program that created it.

PJC: The extension for files created by the now-defunct Master Genealogist software, which can directly import the native file formats of most popular genealogy programs.

PNG: Portable Network Graphics. Developed as a replacement for the GIF format—and used for the same types of files—PNG does a better job of compressing files, resulting in a smaller-size files of equal quality. Most image-editing software can open PNG files.

PSD: Photoshop Document. Adobe Photoshop's native format allows for preservation of layers, masks, and profiles used in image editing.

RAW: Certain digital cameras support this "raw" image format, which uses nearly lossless compression while still being smaller than TIFF format photos. It is sometimes called DNG (Adobe's Digital Negative format).

RMG: RootsMagic genealogy software's native file format.

SIT: A file compressed by StuffIt software. SIT files were originally usable only by Macs, but now Windows can create and open these files, too. Note that both SIT and ZIP shrink the size of other file formats for easier exchanging or archiving. You can click the SIT file icon to "unstuff" the files, but you'll still need the applicable software to view the original files.

TGA: Truevision Advanced Raster Graphics Adapter; used for raster images, such as in video games.

TIFF: Tagged Image File Format. Good for bitmap (pixel-based) images, such as photographs. Since TIFF produces large files, it's excellent if the end use is print (not web) or archival.

TXT: Refers to plain-text files with little formatting; for example, no bold or italics. This format is most commonly used in simple text editors such as Windows Notepad and Mac TextEdit, but you can open them in almost any program that can read a plain-text file (including word processors), making them good for file sharing.

WAV: Short for waveform, WAV is the standard format for storing audio on a PC. You can play WAV files on Windows or Mac in a program such as Windows Media Player or iTunes.

WMA: Windows Media Audio. WMA produces smaller files than WAV, but you can listen to them on similar software, including Windows Media Player and RealPlayer.

WMV: Windows Media Video. Used for internet video, this file format must be read with Windows Media Player or an application such as Real-Player. Flip4Mac offers conversion for Mac users.

ZIP: Similar to SIT, ZIP format uses Zip compression to shrink a document or documents into one smaller file for sharing or archiving. Windows users can create ZIP files using a program such as WINZIP, while Mac OSX users can simply Control-click a file and select Create Archive of [file name].

Computing

Software Comparison Worksheet

You have many genealogy software programs to choose from. For user ratings, visit <**www.gensoftreviews.com**>.

For Mac

Name	Price	Multiple views	Reports	Syncs with FamilySearch.org	Syncs with Ancestry.com
Ancestral Quest <www.ancquest.com>	free "Basics" version; $29.95 (download); $19.95 (upgrade)	●	●		
GEDitCOM II <www.geditcom.com>	$64.99 (license) or $19.99 (upgrade)	●	●		
Family Tree Maker for Mac <www.mackiev.com/ftm/index.html>	$69.95 (download); $29.95 (upgrade from Mac 2 or earlier)	●	●	●	●
Heredis <www.heredis.com/en>	$49.99 (download)	●	●		
iFamily for Mac <www.ifamilyformac.com>	$49	●	●		
Reunion <www.leisterpro.com>	$99 (download/CD) or $54.95 (upgrade)	●	●		
RootsMagic 7 <www.rootsmagic.com>	free "Essentials" version; $29.95 (download); $19.95 (upgrade)	●	●	●	●

Software Comparison Worksheet

For Windows

Name	Price	Multiple views	Reports	Syncs with FamilySearch.org	Syncs with Ancestry.com
Ancestral Quest <www.ancquest.com>	free "Basics" version; $29.95 (download); $19.95 (upgrade)	●	●		
Brother's Keeper <www.bkwin.org>	$45 (CD); $24 (upgrade)	●	●		
Family Historian <www.family-historian.co.uk>	$46.50 (license); $32.29 (upgrade)	●	●		●
Family Tree Maker <www.mackiev.com/ftm/index.html>	$69.95 (download); $29.95 (upgrade from FTM 2012 or earlier)	●	●	●	●
Genbox Family History <www.genbox.com>	$29.95 (license)	●	●		
Heredis <www.heredis.com/en>	$29.99 (download) or $19.99 (upgrade)	●	●		
Legacy Family Tree Deluxe <www.legacyfamilytree.com>	free "Standard" version; $34.95 (download); $39.95 (CD with manual); $26.95 upgrade	●	●		
RootsMagic 7 <www.rootsmagic.com>	free "Essentials" version; $29.95 (download); $19.95 (upgrade)	●	●	●	●

Computing

Genealogy Mobile Apps

Download these apps from the iTunes Store **<www.apple.com/itunes>**, Google Play Store **<play.google.com/store>**, Amazon.com **<www.amazon. com>**, or Windows Phone Store **<www.windowsphone.com/en-us/store/ overview>**.

Allen County Public Library (ACPL Mobile): Search the catalog and see library hours and locations.

Ancestry.com: Edit and upload photos to an Ancestry.com family tree. View your trees, check out "hints," and examine your DNA results.

BillionGraves: Upload and view gravestone photos, along with their geo-tagged locations.

Diigo: See bookmarks, archives, annotations, notes, images, and saved screenshots.

Evernote: Syncs saved content, including text, images, and PDFs.

Facebook: Social networking, plus countless apps and add-ons.

FamilySearch Tree: Search, view, and edit files from the FamilySearch Family Tree on an iPhone.

FamViewer (Aster Software): Supports multiple GEDCOM files and large databases. Works on iOS devices.

Find A Grave: Search or add grave information to an online database.

Flickr: View, upload, and share photos.

GedView: Offers individual and family views. Works with GEDCOM files and supports multiple databases. Works on iOS devices.

Genealogy Gems: Get podcasts and special bonus audio and video content from Lisa Louise Cooke through this app.

GeneDroid: View your Geni family tree on Android devices.

Google: Access the world's largest search engine from your mobile device. Other Google services, such as Gmail, Google Drive, and Google Chrome, have their own apps as well.

HistoryPin: View pictures of historical places uploaded by other users, or pin your own.

Library of Congress: Get a virtual tour of the library.

MobileFamilyTree (Synium Software GmbH): View your MacFamilyTree data on iOS devices.

MyHeritage: View and edit trees, search records, and examine your DNA results.

Pinterest: "Pin" (bookmark) links and pictures and organize them onto boards, plus view and save others' pins.

TribalPages: Create, update, and share your family tree.

World Family Tree: View your Geni family tree on iOS and Android devices.

CENSUS

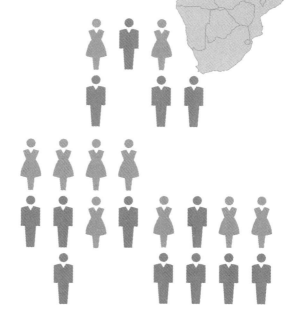

Most Common Ancestries in the United States, 2016

Ancestry	Number of people	Percentage of population
German	45.8 million	14.4%
Irish	33.1 million	10.4%
English	24.4 million	7.7%
American	21.9 million	6.9%
Italian	17.1 million	5.4%
Polish	9.3 million	2.9%
French	8.1 million	2.6%
Scottish	5.4 million	1.7%
Norwegian	4.4 million	1.4%
Dutch	4.2 million	1.3%
Swedish	3.9 million	1.2%
Subsaharan African	3.2 million	1.0%
Scotch-Irish	3.0 million	1.0%
West Indian	2.8 million	0.9%
Russian	2.8 million	0.9%
French Canadian	2.1 million	0.7%

Census

Historical US Populations
in Millions

1790: 3.9

1800: 5.2

1810: 7.0

1820: 10.0

1830: 12.8

1840: 17.0

1850: 23.0

1860: 31.4

1870: 38.6

1880: 50.2

1890: 63.0

1900: 76.2

1910: 92.2

1920: 106.0

1930: 123.2

1940: 132.2

1950: 151.3

1960: 179.3

1970: 203.2

1980: 226.5

1990: 248.7

2000: 281.4

2010: 309.3

US Census Records Websites

$ = subscription required to access most records

$ Ancestry.com <www.ancestry.com>
All extant population census records and every-name indexes

$ Archives.com <www.archives.com>
Partial index and records for 1870, 1880, 1900, and 1910 censuses; index for 1860 and 1930 censuses (additional indexes are being added)

Census-Online.com <www.census-online.com>
State-by-state directory for free digitized federal censuses and other kinds of records. Many link to USGenWeb; coverage and availability vary by state

$ CensusRecords.com <www.censusrecords.com>
Images and indexes for all censuses 1790–1940. The 1940 census is available for free

FamilySearch.org <www.familysearch.org>
Every-name indexes for all US federal censuses, and images for all except 1880 and 1930

$ Findmypast <www.findmypast.com>
Indexes and images for all US censuses; 1940 census is available for free

$ Fold3 <www.fold3.com>
Records and every-name indexes for 1860, 1930, and portions of 1900 to 1920 (this site will eventually add all US census records)

HeritageQuest Online <www.heritagequestonline.com>
Record images for all US censuses; head-of-household indexes for 1790 to 1820, 1860 to 1920, and part of 1930 (available through subscribing libraries)

Internet Archive <archive.org/details/us_census>
Images of 1790–1930 federal censuses, scanned from the Allen County Public Library's collection

USGenWeb Archives Census Project <usgwarchives.net/census>
Volunteer-submitted indexes and some images of census records from various places and years

Online Census Search Tips

★ **Read the site's search tips and instructions**. These will reveal tricks such as using wildcard symbols to find alternate spellings of your ancestors' names.

★ **Search a site's individual census databases one at a time**. Those customized search forms often let you include terms not allowed in a site's global search, helping you better target your search.

★ **Make sure the collection covers the right time and place**. Go to the page for the individual census database and look for background information. You might learn the collection doesn't contain all extant census schedules, or that the place where your ancestor lived wasn't indexed or wasn't included in that enumeration.

★ **Try different search fields**. Start by entering all you know about the person. If you don't get results, search on fewer terms and combinations of terms.

★ **Seek alternate name spellings**. A census taker or indexer might've interpreted the name so outlandishly that a "sounds like" search wouldn't pick up on the misspelling.

★ **Leave out the name**. Instead of a name, search on variables such as residence, birth date and place, place of origin, and immigration date.

★ **Be flexible**. Your ancestor might've lived in a place you didn't expect, or he might have reported a different age or birthplace from the one you were looking for. Use date ranges and try leaving some fields blank to account for uncertainty.

★ **Browse**. Navigate to schedules for the census year and the enumeration district (ED) where you think your ancestor lived (you can use the ED tools at <www.stevemorse.org> to determine the enumeration district). Then, examine the records page by page.

Questions in the Census

Name of head of family

Free white males 16 years and older, including heads of family

Free white males under 16 years

Number of free white females

Number of all other free persons

Number of slaves

Dwellings and miscellaneous

1800 AND **1810** CENSUS QUESTIONS

Name of head of family

Number of free white males under age 10

Number of free white males of 10 and under 16

Number of free white males of 16 and under 26

Number of free white males of 26 and under 45

Number of free white males of 45 and up

Number of free white females under age 10

Number of free white females of 10 and under 16

Number of free white females of 16 and under 26

Number of free white females of 26 and under 45

Number of free white females of 45 and up

Number of all other persons except Indians not taxed

Number of slaves

1820 CENSUS QUESTIONS

Name of head of family

Number of free white males under age 10

Number of free white males 10 to 16

Number of free white males 16 to 18

Number of free white males 16 to 26

Number of free white males 26 to 45

Number of free white males 45 and up

Number of free white females under age 10

Number of free white females 10 to 16

Number of free white females 16 to 26

Number of free white females 26 to 45

Number of free white females 45 and up

Number of foreigners not naturalized

Number of persons engaged in agriculture

Number of persons engaged in commerce

Number of persons engaged in manufacturing

Number of free colored males to age 14

Number of free colored males 14 to 26

Number of free colored males 26 to 45

Number of free colored males 45 and up

Number of free colored females to age 14

Number of free colored females 14 to 26

Number of free colored females 26 to 45

Number of free colored females 45 and up

Number of all other persons

Number of slaves

1830 CENSUS QUESTIONS

PAGE 1

Name of head of family

Number of free white males under age 5

Number of free white males age 5 to 10

Number of free white males age 10 to 15

Number of free white males age 15 to 20

Number of free white males age 20 to 30

Number of free white males age 30 to 40

Number of free white males age 40 to 50

Number of free white males age 50 to 60

Number of free white males age 60 to 70

Number of free white males age 70 to 80

Number of free white males age 80 to 90

Number of free white males age 90 to 100

Number of free white males age 100 and up

Number of free white females under age 5

Number of free white females age 5 to 10

Number of free white females age 10 to 15

Number of free white females age 15 to 20

Number of free white females age 20 to 30

Number of free white females age 30 to 40

Number of free white females age 40 to 50

Number of free white females age 50 to 60

Number of free white females age 60 to 70

Number of free white females age 70 to 80

Number of free white females age 80 to 90

Number of free white females age 90 to 100

Number of free white females age 100 and up

PAGE 2

Name of head of family

Number of male slaves under age 10

Number of male slaves age 10 to 24

Number of male slaves age 24 to 36

Number of male slaves age 36 to 55

Number of male slaves age 55 to 100

Number of male slaves age 100 and up

Number of female slaves under age 10

Number of female slaves age 10 to 24

Number of female slaves age 24 to 36

Number of female slaves age 36 to 55

Number of female slaves age 55 to 100

Number of female slaves age 100 and up

Number of free colored males under age 10

Number of free colored males age 10 to 24

Number of free colored males age 24 to 36

Number of free colored males age 36 to 55

Number of free colored males age 55 to 100

Number of free colored males age 100 and up

Number of free colored females under age 10

Number of free colored females age 10 to 24

Number of free colored females age 24 to 36

Number of free colored females age 36 to 55

Number of free colored females age 55 to 100

Number of free colored females age 100 and up

TOTAL

White persons deaf and dumb under age 14

White persons deaf and dumb age 14 to 25

White persons deaf and dumb age 25 and up

White persons blind

White foreigners not naturalized

Slaves and colored persons deaf and dumb under age 14

Slaves and colored persons deaf and dumb age 14 to 25

Slaves and colored persons deaf and dumb age 25 and up

Slaves and colored persons blind

1840 CENSUS QUESTIONS

PAGE 1

Name of head of family

Number of free white males under age 5

Number of free white males age 5 to 10

Number of free white males age 10 to 15

Number of free white males age 15 to 20

Number of free white males age 20 to 30

Number of free white males age 30 to 40

Number of free white males age 40 to 50

Number of free white males age 50 to 60

Number of free white males age 60 to 70

Number of free white males age 70 to 80

Number of free white males age 80 to 90

Number of free white males age 90 to 100

Number of free white males age 100 and up

Number of free white females under age 5

Number of free white females age 5 to 10

Number of free white females age 10 to 15

Number of free white females age 15 to 20

Number of free white females age 20 to 30

Number of free white females age 30 to 40

Number of free white females age 40 to 50

Number of free white females age 50 to 60

Number of free white females age 60 to 70

Number of free white females age 70 to 80

Number of free white females age 80 to 90

Number of free white females age 90 to 100

Number of free white females age 100 and up

PAGE 2

Name of head of family

Number of male slaves under age 10

Number of male slaves age 10 to 24

Number of male slaves age 24 to 36

Number of male slaves age 36 to 55

Number of male slaves age 55 to 100

Number of male slaves age 100 and up

Number of female slaves under age 10

Number of female slaves age 10 to 24

Number of female slaves age 24 to 36

Number of female slaves age 36 to 55

Number of female slaves age 55 to 100

Number of female slaves age 100 and up

Number of free colored males under age 10

Number of free colored males age 10 to 24

Number of free colored males age 24 to 36

Number of free colored males age 36 to 55

Number of free colored males age 55 to 100

Number of free colored males age 100 and up

Number of free colored females under age 10

Number of free colored females age 10 to 24

Number of free colored females age 24 to 36

Number of free colored females age 36 to 55

Number of free colored females age 55 to 100

Number of free colored females age 100 and up

TOTAL

Number of persons employed in mining

Number of persons employed in agriculture

Number of persons employed in commerce

Number of persons employed in manufacturing and trades

Number of persons employed in ocean navigation

Number of persons employed in canal, lake, river navigation

Number of persons employed in learned prof'ns and engineers

Revolutionary or military service pensioner's name

Revolutionary or military service pensioner's age

White persons deaf and dumb under age 14

White persons deaf and dumb age 14 to 25

White persons deaf and dumb age 25 and up

White persons blind

White persons insane and idiots at public charge

White persons insane and idiots at private charge

Slaves and colored persons deaf and dumb under age 14

Slaves and colored persons deaf and dumb age 14 to 25

Slaves and colored persons deaf and dumb age 25 and up

Slaves and colored persons blind

Slaves and colored persons insane and idiots at public charge

Slaves and colored persons insane and idiots at private charge

1850 CENSUS QUESTIONS

1. Dwelling number
2. Family number
3. Name of every person whose usual place of abode on June 1, 1850, was with this family
4. Age
5. Sex
6. Color
7. Profession, occupation, or trade of each male over 15
8. Value of real estate owned
9. Place of birth
10. Married within the year
11. In school within the year
12. Persons over 20 unable to read and write
13. If deaf and dumb, blind, insane, idiot, pauper, or convict

1850 CENSUS SLAVE SCHEDULE QUESTIONS

1. Name of slave owners
2. Number of slaves
3. Age
4. Sex
5. Color
6. Fugitives from the state
7. Number manumitted
8. Deaf and dumb, blind, insane, or idiotic

1. Dwelling number
2. Family number
3. Name of every person whose usual place of abode on June 1, 1860, was with this family
4. Age
5. Sex
6. Color
7. Profession, occupation, or trade of each person over 15
8. Value of real estate owned
9. Value of personal estate owned
10. Place of birth
11. Married within the year
12. In school within the year
13. Persons over 20 unable to read and write
14. If deaf and dumb, blind, insane, idiot, pauper, or convict

1860 CENSUS SLAVE SCHEDULE QUESTIONS

1. Name of slave owners
2. Number of slaves
3. Age
4. Sex
5. Color
6. Fugitives from the state
7. Number manumitted
8. Deaf and dumb, blind, insane, or idiotic

1870 CENSUS QUESTIONS

1. Dwelling number
2. Family number
3. Name of every person whose usual place of abode on June 1, 1870, was with this family

4. Age

5. Sex

6. Color

7. Profession, occupation, or trade

8. Value of real estate owned

9. Value of personal estate owned

10. Place of birth

11. Father foreign-born

12. Mother foreign-born

13. Month born within the year

14. Month married within the year

15. In school within the year

16. Cannot read

17. Cannot write

18. Deaf and dumb, blind, insane, or idiotic

19. Male citizen of 21

20. Males not eligible to vote

1880 CENSUS QUESTIONS

Street name

House number

1. Dwelling number

2. Family number

3. Name of every person whose usual place of abode on June 1, 1880, was with this family

4. Color

5. Sex

6. Age

7. Month born if during census year

8. Relationship to head of household

9. Single

10. Married

11. Widowed/divorced

12. Married during year

13. Profession, occupation, or trade

14. Months unemployed this year

15. Currently ill? If so, specify.

16. Blind

17. Deaf and dumb

18. Idiotic

19. Insane

20. Disabled

21. School this year

22. Cannot read

23. Cannot write

24. Birthplace

25. Birthplace of father

26. Birthplace of mother

1890 CENSUS QUESTIONS

Lost to fire except for fragments, the 1890 forms added questions about how long a person had lived in the United States and his or her naturalization status. This enumeration also included the column "mother of how many children" and how many of those children were living. The 1890 census included a veterans schedule for enumerating veterans of the Civil War and their widows; about half of these schedules survived and can substitute for the lost census if you're lucky enough to have a Union soldier in the family.

1900 CENSUS QUESTIONS

Street

House number

1. Dwelling number

2. Family number

3. Name of every person whose usual place of abode on June 1, 1900, was with this family

4. Relationship to head of family

5. Color

6. Sex

7. Birth month and year

8. Age

9. Marital status

10. Number of years married

11. Mother of how many children?

12. Number of these children living

13. Birthplace of this person

14. Birthplace of this person's father

15. Birthplace of this person's mother

16. Year of immigration

17. Number of years in US

18. Naturalized citizen

19. Occupation of every person 10 and older

20. Months not employed

21. Months in school

22. Can read

23. Can write

24. Speaks English

25. Owned or rented

26. Owned free or mortgage

27. Farm or house

28. Number of farm schedule

1910 CENSUS QUESTIONS

Street

Home number

1. Dwelling number

2. Family number

3. Name of every person whose usual place of abode on April 15, 1910, was with this family

4. Relationship

5. Sex
6. Color
7. Age
8. Marital status
9. Number of years—present marriage
10. Mother of how many children?
11. Number of living children
12. Birthplace of this person
13. Birthplace of this person's father
14. Birthplace of this person's mother
15. Year of immigration
16. Naturalized citizen or alien?
17. Speak English? If not, give name of language.
18. Profession or occupation
19. Nature of business
20. Employer or wage earner or working on own account
21. Out of work April 15, 1910
22. No. of weeks out of work in 1909
23. Can read
24. Can write
25. School since September 1, 1909
26. Owned/rented
27. Owned free or mortgaged
28. Farm or house
29. No. of farm schedule
30. Civil War veteran
31. Blind
32. Deaf and dumb

1920 CENSUS QUESTIONS

1. Street
2. Home number

3. Dwelling number

4. Family number

5. Name of each person whose place of abode on January 1, 1920, was in this family

6. Relationship

7. Own or rent home

8. Owned free or mortgaged

9. Sex

10. Color or race

11. Age

12. Marital status

13. Immigration year

14. Naturalized or alien

15. Naturalization year

16. School since September 1, 1919

17. Can read

18. Can write

19. Birthplace of this person

20. Mother tongue

21. Birthplace of father

22. Mother tongue

23. Birthplace of mother

24. Mother tongue

25. Speaks English

26. Profession or occupation

27. Nature of business

28. Employer, wage earner or self-employed

29. Number of farm schedule

1930 CENSUS QUESTIONS

1. Street

2. Home number

3. Dwelling number

4. Family number

5. Name of every person whose place of abode on April 1, 1930, was in this family

6. Relationship to head of family

7. Own or rent home

8. Value of home or monthly rental

9. Radio set

10. Family live on farm a year ago?

11. Sex

12. Color or race

13. Age at last birthday

14. Marital condition

15. Age at first marriage

16. School since September 1, 1929

17. Can read and write

18. Birthplace of this person

19. Birthplace of this person's father

20. Birthplace of this person's mother

21. Language spoken in home before coming to United States

22. Immigration year

23. Naturalization

24. Speaks English

25. Occupation

26. Industry

27. Class of worker

28. Actually at work yesterday or last working day?

29. Line number for unemployed

30. Veteran

31. Which war or expedition

32. Number of farm schedule

1. Street

2. House number

3. Family number

4. Home owned or rented

5. Value of home if owned or monthly rental if rented

6. Does this household live on a farm

7. Name of each person whose usual place of residence on April 1, 1940, was in this household

8. Relation to head of household

9. Sex

10. Color or race

11. Age at last birthday

12. Marital status

13. Attended school or college any time since March 1, 1940?

14. Highest grade of school completed

15. Place of birth

16. Citizenship of the foreign born

17. City, town, or village

18. County

19. State (or territory or foreign country)

20. On a farm?

21. Was this person at work for pay or profit in private or nonemergency government work during week of March 24-30?

22. If not, was he at work on or assigned to public emergency work (WPA, NYA, CCC, etc.) during week of March 24-30?

23. Was this person seeking work?

24. If not seeking work, did he have a job, business, etc.?

25. Indicate whether engaged in home housework, in school, unable to work or other

26. If at private or nonemergency work, number of hours worked during week of March 24-30?

27. If seeking work or assigned to public emergency work, duration of unemployment up to March 30, 1940—in weeks

28. Occupation

29. Industry

30. Class of worker

31. Number of weeks worked in 1939

32. Amount of money wages or salary received (including commissions)

33. Did this person receive income of $50 or more from sources other than money wages or salary?

34. Number of farm schedule

35. Name

36. Place of birth of father

37. Place of birth of mother

38. Mother tongue

39. Veteran

40. If child, is veteran-father dead (yes or no)

41. War or military service

42. Does this person have a federal Social Security Number?

43. Were deductions for federal Old-Age insurance or railroad retirement made from this person's wages or salary in 1939?

44. If so, were deductions made from (1) all, (2) one-half or more, (3) part but less than half of wages or salary?

45. Usual occupation

46. Usual industry

47. Usual class of worker

48. Has this woman been married more than once?

49. Age at first marriage

50. Number of children ever born

Census Questions by Category

NAME

Head of household: 1790, 1800, 1810, 1820, 1830, 1840

Everyone in the household (except slaves): from 1850 on

BIRTH DATE AND PLACE

Age range of free white males (ranges differ): 1790, 1800, 1810, 1820, 1830, 1840

Age range of free white females (ranges differ): 1800, 1810, 1820, 1830, 1840

Age of everyone in the household: 1850 on

Birthplace: 1850 on

Born within the census year (with month): 1870, 1880

Month and year of birth: 1900

PARENTS

Foreign-born parents: 1870

Parents' place of birth: 1880 on

Mother tongue: 1910, 1940

Self and parents' mother tongue: 1920, 1930

MARRIAGE

Married within the census year: 1850, 1860, 1870 (includes the month), 1880, 1890

Marital status: 1880 on

Number of years married: 1900, 1910

Age at first marriage: 1930

IMMIGRATION AND CITIZENSHIP

Number of aliens/persons not naturalized: 1820, 1830, 1840

Year of immigration to United States: 1900, 1910, 1920, 1930

Number of years in United States: 1890, 1900

Naturalization status: 1870 (for males over 21), 1890 on

PHYSICAL OR MENTAL HEALTH

Persons in household who were blind, deaf, or dumb: 1830, 1840, 1850, 1860, 1870, 1880, 1890, 1910

Persons in household who were idiotic or insane: 1850, 1860, 1870, 1880

Mother of how many children/number living: 1890, 1900, 1910

Whether suffering from chronic disease: 1890

PERSONAL PROPERTY

Value of real estate owned: 1850, 1860, 1870

Value of personal estate: 1860, 1870

Own or rent home: 1900, 1910, 1920, 1930, 1940

Had a radio: 1930

EDUCATION/OCCUPATION

Number of persons (including slaves) engaged in agriculture, commerce, or manufacturing: 1820

Occupation: 1840 on

Attended school in the past year: 1840 on

Can read or write: 1850 on

Income: 1940

OTHER

Number of free colored: 1820, 1830, 1840

Color/race: 1850 on

Relationship to head of household: 1880 on

Able to speak English: 1900, 1910, 1920, 1930

Veteran status: 1910 (Civil War only), 1930, 1940

Pensioner for Revolutionary or military service: 1840

If person is a pauper, convict, or homeless child: 1850, 1860, 1890

Eligibility to vote: 1870

Whether assigned a Social Security number: 1940

Census Abbreviations

RELATIONSHIPS

A aunt

Ad adopted

AdCl adopted child

AdD adopted daughter

AdGcl adopted grandchild

AdM adopted mother

AdS adopted son

B brother

Bl or **Bil** brother-in-law

Bo boarder

C cousin

D daughter

DL or **DIL** daughter-in-law

F father

Fl or **Fil** father-in-law

Gf grandfather

Gm grandmother

Gua guardian

h husband

L lodger

ml or **mil** mother-in-law

R roomer

s son

sf stepfather

si sister

SL son-in-law

sm stepmother

ss stepson

ten tenant

u uncle

vi visitor

w wife

CITIZENSHIP STATUS

AL alien (not naturalized)

NA naturalized

NR not recorded

PA declaration of intent filed

COLOR/ETHNICITY

⅛ octoroon (one-eighth African ancestry)

¼ quadroon (one-fourth African ancestry)

B black

Ch Chinese

M or **Mu** Mulatto

In Indian

Jp Japanese

Ot other

W white

OCCUPATIONS

Ap apprentice

Asst assistant

At attendant

Bu butler

Cap captain

Cha chamber maid

Dla day laborer

Dom domestic

Emp employee

En engineer

FaH farm hand

FaL farm laborer

FaW farm worker

Go governess

h.gi hired girl

H.H hired hand

Hk housekeeper

H.Maid housemaid

La laborer

lau laundry

man manager

Nu nurse

Ph doctor

Sa sailor

Se servant

wa warden

wkm workman

wt waiter

MILITARY

CA Survivor of the Confederate Army

CN Survivor of the Confederate Navy

UA Survivor of the Union Army

UN Survivor of the Union Navy

Non-Population Schedules

Schedules of defective, dependent, and delinquent classes: 1880

Agricultural censuses: 1850, 1860, 1870, 1880

Manufacturing and industry schedules: 1810, 1820, 1850, 1860, 1870, 1880

Slave schedules: 1850, 1860

Mortality schedules: 1850, 1860, 1870, 1880, 1885 (some areas), 1900 (Minnesota only)

US state/territorial census: 1885 (some areas)

Social statistics schedules: 1850, 1860, 1870, 1885

Indian schedules: 1880, 1900, 1910

Indian reservation censuses: 1885 to 1940

Indian school censuses: 1910 to 1939

Revolutionary War pensioners: 1840

Civil War veterans schedules: 1890 (extant for half of Kentucky and beginning with L through W)

Schedules of military personnel on bases and vessels (including overseas): 1900, 1910, 1920

Schedules of merchant seamen on vessels: 1930

State and Territorial Censuses

Throughout history, US states have variously administered their own censuses. These can be useful by providing information about your ancestors between federal censuses, or by filling in gaps left by missing federal census records. Learn where to find state census records (and which survive) on the FamilySearch Wiki **<www.familysearch.org/wiki/en/Main_Page>**.

State	State and territorial census year(s)
Alabama	1816, 1818, 1820-21, 1823, 1850, 1855, 1866, 1907
Alaska	1870, 1878-79, 1881, 1885, 1887, 1890-95, 1904-07, 1914, 1917
Arizona	1866-67, 1869, 1872, 1874, 1876, 1880, 1882
Arkansas	1823, 1829, 1865, 1911
California	1788, 1790, 1796-98, 1816, 1836, 1844, 1852
Colorado	1860, 1866, 1885
Connecticut	None known
Delaware	1782
District of Columbia	1803, 1867, 1878
Florida	1825, 1855, 1866-68, 1875, 1885, 1895, 1935, 1945
Georgia	1798-1800, 1827, 1834, 1838, 1845, 1852-53, 1859, 1865, 1879
Hawaii	1866, 1878, 1890, 1896
Idaho	None known
Illinois	1810, 1818, 1820, 1825, 1830, 1835, 1840, 1845, 1855, 1865
Indiana	1807, 1853, 1857, 1866, 1871, 1877, 1883, 1889, 1901, 1907, 1913, 1919, 1925, 1931, 1937
Iowa	1836, 1838, 1844, 1846, 1847, 1849, 1851-52, 1854, 1856, 1859, 1885, 1895, 1905, 1915, 1925
Kansas	1855, 1865, 1875, 1885, 1895, 1905, 1915, 1925
Kentucky	None known
Louisiana	None known (though several colonial censuses from 1699-1796)
Maine	1837
Maryland	1776, 1778
Massachusetts	1855, 1865

State	State and territorial census year(s)
Michigan	1837, 1845, 1854, 1864, 1874, 1884, 1894
Minnesota	1849, 1853, 1855, 1857, 1865, 1875, 1885, 1895, 1905
Mississippi	1801, 1805, 1808–1810, 1816, 1818, 1820, 1822–25, 1830, 1833, 1837, 1840–41, 1845, 1850, 1853, 1860, 1866
Missouri	1817, 1819, 1840, 1844, 1852, 1856, 1860, 1864, 1876, 1880
Montana	None known
Nebraska	1854–56, 1865, 1869, 1885
Nevada	1860–61, 1862–63, 1875
New Hampshire	None known
New Jersey	1855, 1865, 1875, 1885, 1895, 1905, 1915
New Mexico	1790, 1823, 1845, 1885
New York	1790, 1825, 1835, 1845, 1855, 1865, 1875, 1892, 1905, 1915, 1925
North Carolina	1784–87
North Dakota	1885, 1915, 1925
Ohio	None known
Oklahoma	1890, 1907
Oregon	1842–46, 1849–50, 1853–59, 1865, 1870, 1875, 1885, 1895, 1905
Pennsylvania	None known
Rhode Island	1774, 1777, 1782, 1865, 1875, 1885, 1905, 1915, 1925, 1935
South Carolina	1829, 1839, 1869, 1875
South Dakota	1885, 1895, 1905, 1915, 1925, 1935, 1945
Tennessee	1891
Texas	1829–1836
Utah	1851, 1856
Vermont	None known
Virginia	1782–86
Washington	1856–58, 1860, 1871, 1877–81, 1883, 1885, 1887, 1889, 1892, 1898
West Virginia	None known
Wisconsin	1836, 1838, 1842, 1846, 1847, 1855, 1865, 1875, 1885, 1895, 1905
Wyoming	1869

8

IMMIGRATION

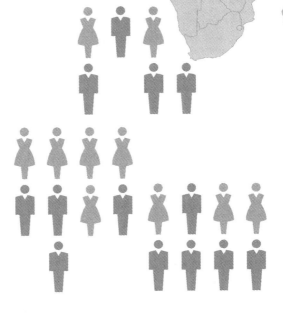

US Immigrants by Country, 1820–1975

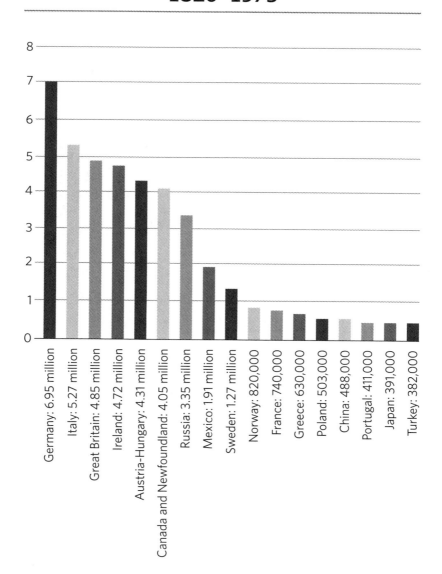

Timeline of Emigration
Push and Pull Factors

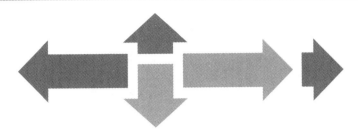

1845 The Great Famine strikes Ireland, starving 1 million Irishmen and forcing another 1.5 million to emigrate over the next several years.

1848 Revolutions in Germany and across Central Europe force political dissidents to flee the country. At the same time, miners discover gold in California, sparking the California Gold Rush and attracting miners from around the world.

1860s More than 100,000 Swedes immigrate to the United States after years of poor harvests, droughts, and floods.

1905 Pogroms against Jewish communities in Eastern Europe (notably, in Russia) intensify, driving Jews to emigrate to America.

1906 Mount Vesuvius in Italy erupts. An earthquake two years later rocks the southern Italian peninsula and triggers a tsunami, killing nearly 200,000 people and driving millions to leave Italy.

1917 The February Revolution overthrows the Russian tsar. Over the next several years, anarchists, czarist aristocrats, intellectuals, and other political dissidents emigrate to other places around the world.

Timeline of Immigration Laws

1790 US establishes uniform naturalization rules for white males 21 and older; children of naturalized citizens get automatic citizenship.

1795 Free white females age 21 and older can become citizens.

1804 Widows and children can become citizens if the husband or father died before filing final papers.

1824 Alien minors, upon turning 21, can be naturalized if they've lived in the United States for five years.

1848 The United States expands westward with the Treaty of Guadalupe Hidalgo, extending citizenship to thousands of residents in the New Mexico Territory and California.

1855 Alien women can become citizens upon marrying US citizens.

1862 Aliens who've received honorable discharges from the US Army can skip filing declarations of intention.

1868 The Fourteenth Amendment declares former slaves citizens.

1870 People of African descent may become citizens.

1882 The Chinese Exclusion Act passes, severly limiting immigration from China.

1887 The Dawes Act entitles American Indians who've accepted land allotments to become citizens.

1891 The Bureau of Immigration is established.

1894 Declarations of intention are waived for aliens who are honorably discharged after five years in the Navy or Marine Corps.

1906 The Bureau of Immigration and Naturalization Service (INS) is established. Immigration to the United States peaks the next year.

1917 Puerto Ricans become US citizens. That same year, Congress passes a sweeping law barring immigration from most of east and south Asia, the Middle East, and the Pacific Islands. The law also establishes a literacy requirement.

1921 The US Emergency Quota Act passes, limiting annual immigration from each country to 3 percent of the US population from that place.

1922 Married women's citizenship becomes independent of their husbands'.

1924 American Indians are granted full citizenship; the quotas outlined in the Emergency Quota Act are revised to reduce immigration from 3 percent to 2 percent.

1929 Photographs are required on petition for naturalization.

1940 The Alien Registration Act requires non-naturalized aliens to register with the government.

1943 Asian immigrants can become citizens.

1952 The Immigration and Naturalization Act of 1952 revises immigration law in the United States, and it continues to govern immigration and citizenship today. The age requirement for naturalization drops to eighteen, and declarations of intention become optional.

1990 Courts no longer naturalize citizens.

2003 The INS becomes US Citizenship and Immigration Services.

Passenger List Availability for Busiest US Ports

PASSENGER LIST	AVAILABILITY
Baltimore	1820–1897, 1891–1957
Beaufort, North Carolina	1865
Boston	1820–1874, 1883–1891, 1891–1943
Bridgeport, Connecticut	1870, 1929–1959
Charleston, South Carolina	1820–1829, 1865, 1890–1939
Galveston, Texas	1846–1951
Gloucester, Massachusetts	1820, 1832–1839, 1867–1868, 1870, 1906–1943
Gulfport and Pascagoula, Mississippi	1903–1954
Key West, Florida	1837–1852, 1857–1868, 1890–1945
New Bedford, Massachusetts	1822, 1825–1852, 1902–1954
New London, Connecticut	1820–1847, 1929–1959
New Orleans	1813–1952
Newport, Rhode Island	1820–1852, 1857
New York City	1789–1957
Norfolk and Portsmouth, Virginia	1820–1857
Pensacola, Florida	1890–1948
Philadelphia	1800–1882, 1883–1948
Portland, Maine	1893–1943
Providence, Rhode Island	1820–1867, 1911–1954
San Francisco	1882–1957
Savannah, Georgia	1820–1826, 1831, 1847–1851, 1865–1868, 1890–1945
Seattle	1882–1957
Wilmington, Delaware	1820, 1830–1831, 1833, 1840–1849
US–Canada border	1895–1956
US–Mexico border	1903–1950s

Passenger Search Tips

⭐ **Look for clues in census records**. US censuses from 1900 to 1930 give the year of immigration and indicate whether someone is naturalized. Many censuses also provide a birthplace (usually a country).

⭐ **Try to find out the person's name at birth**, which is how he'll probably appear on passenger lists. Many immigrants changed their names after arrival to sound more "American."

⭐ **Search for alternate name spellings**. The name may have been mistranscribed or misindexed, your ancestor may have altered the spelling, or the ship's clerk may have written it down incorrectly.

⭐ **Search immigration and emigration collections** on websites such as Ancestry.com **<www.ancestry.com>** (by subscription), the National Archives' Access to Archival Databases **<aad.archives.gov>**, Ellis Island **<www.libertyellisfoundation.org>**, Castle Garden **<www.castlegarden. org>**, FamilySearch.org **<www.familysearch.org>**, and the Immigrant Ships Transcribers' Guild **<www.immigrantships.net>**.

⭐ **Search for women under both their maiden and married names**. If you can't find a mother, look for her children.

⭐ **Search for your ancestor's neighbors and friends on passenger lists**, since many immigrants traveled and settled with those from their hometowns.

⭐ **Browse passenger records for the arrival date or year** using an online collection or a tool such Steve Morse's One-Step search site **<stevemorse.org>**.

⭐ **Check naturalization records for an immigrant's birth name**. These records are available through the USCIS Genealogy Service **<www. uscis.gov/genealogy>** for 1906 and later years; records for various years and locales are available on Ancestry.com, Fold3 **<www.fold3.com>**, and FamilySearch.org.

Passenger List
Notations and Abbreviations

admitted passenger allowed to enter the United States

c or **NAT followed by numbers** passenger's naturalization certificate file number

C/A certificate of arrival

dcd discharged

Deported passenger refused entry and returned home

in hospital immigrant was hospitalized for illness; an outcome may note the passenger was discharged, deported or died in the hospital

LPC likely public charge

name lined out passenger's name was changed or corrected; the corrected name is written in

nob, **not shipped**, or **passenger's entry lined out** not on board; passenger didn't board the ship or was re-recorded elsewhere on the list (may be due to an incorrectly recorded cabin class)

si passenger was referred to the Board of Special Inquiry for further evaluation

transit passenger was en route to another country or did not plan to stay in the United States

USB US-born

USC US citizen

X, **D**, or **Held** passenger was detained at the port of entry

Timeline of European Territorial Changes

1648 The Thirty Years' War ends, resulting in the rise of France and Sweden and in the decentralization of the Holy Roman Empire.

1713 The War of the Spanish Succession prevents the union of France and Spain; Spain cedes parts of the Netherlands and Italy to Austria.

1772 Poland undergoes the first of its three Partitions, in which its neighbors annex Polish land and remove it from the map. The other Partitions take place in 1793 and 1795.

1815 The Congress of Vienna ends the Napoleonic Wars, stripping France's territorial gains, dissolving the Holy Roman Empire, and laying the foundation for German and Italian unification.

1871 The various German states combine into one German Empire. That same year, the Kingdom of Italy incorporates Rome as its capital, ending the decade's-long process of Italian unification.

1919 The Treaty of Versailles dismantles Austria-Hungary and redraws Central European borders after World War I.

1921 Southern Ireland becomes the Irish Free State; six northern countries remain part of the United Kingdom (now Northern Ireland).

1945–47 The Potsdam Conference and the Paris Peace Treaties end World War II, with restoration of most pre-war borders and a division of Europe into the Soviet-controlled Eastern Bloc and the US-allied Western Bloc, spawning the Cold War.

1989–91 Revolutions in Eastern Bloc countries result in the fall of Communism and dissolution of the Soviet Union.

Europe, 1714

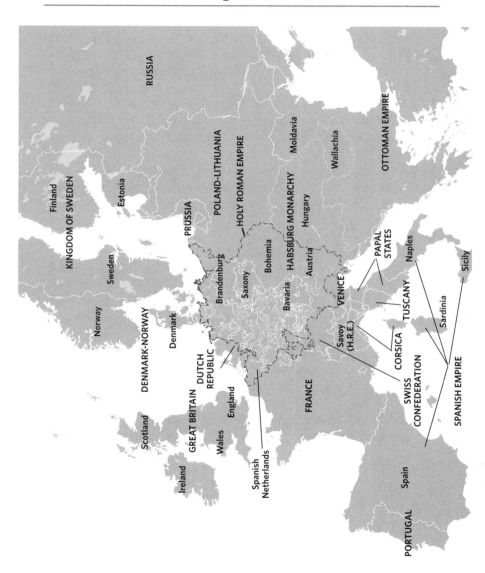

Europe, 1815

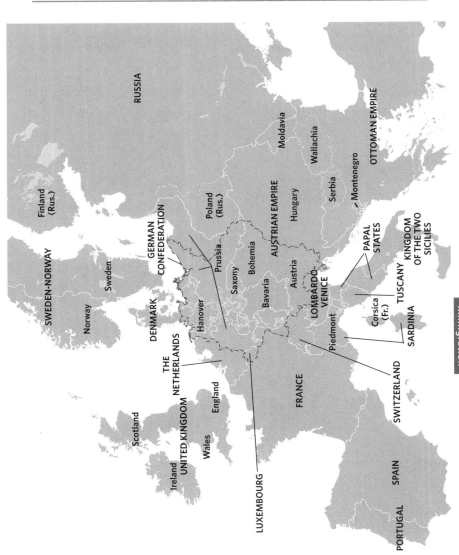

Immigration

Europe, 1890

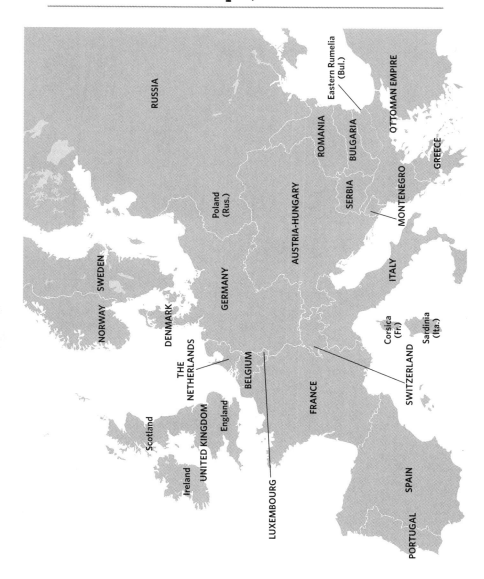

Europe, 1914

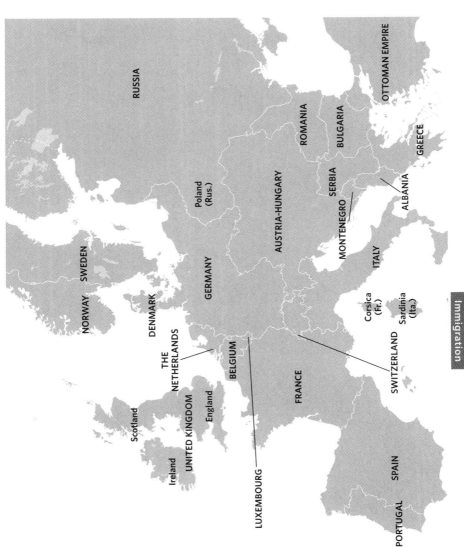

RUSSIA

OTTOMAN EMPIRE

ROMANIA

BULGARIA

GREECE

Poland (Rus.)

AUSTRIA-HUNGARY

SERBIA

ALBANIA

MONTENEGRO

SWEDEN

ITALY

NORWAY

GERMANY

DENMARK

Corsica (Fr.)

Sardinia (Ita.)

THE NETHERLANDS

BELGIUM

SWITZERLAND

Scotland

UNITED KINGDOM

England

FRANCE

Ireland

LUXEMBOURG

SPAIN

PORTUGAL

Immigration

Europe, 1928

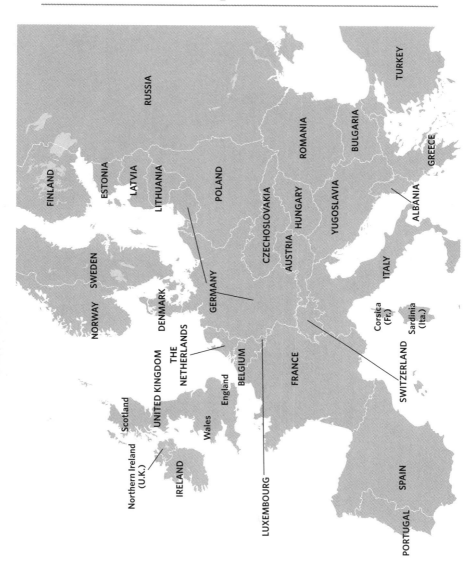

Europe, 1956

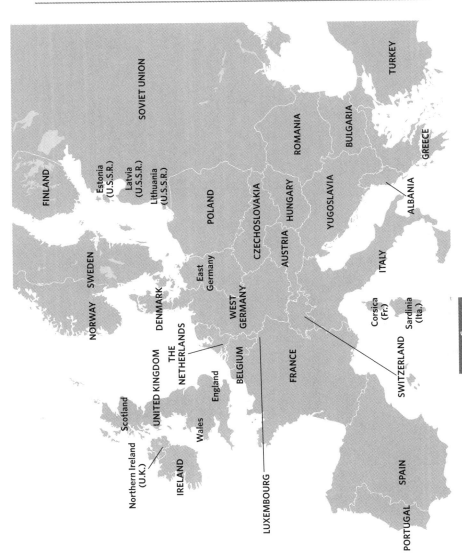

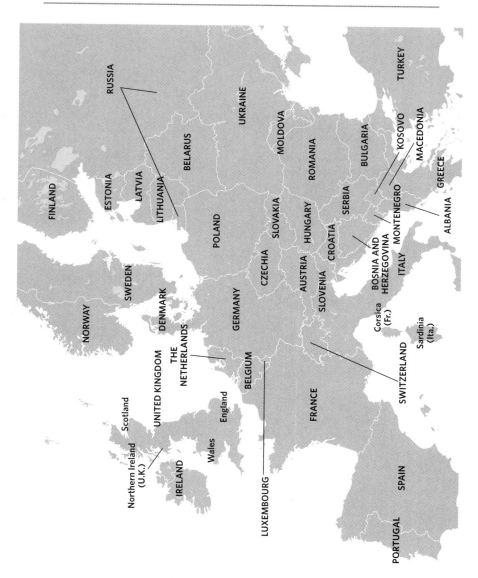

9

MILITARY

Timeline of US Military Conflicts

1622–1646 **Powhatan Wars**: Jamestown settlers and Powhatan Indians clash.

1637 **Pequot War**: Pequot Indians and Puritan settlers battle in the Connecticut River Valley.

1675–1678 **King Philip's War**: Indian leader Metacomet (a.k.a. King Philip) organizes New England tribes in a revolt against Colonial expansion.

1676 **Bacon's Rebellion**: Nathaniel Bacon leads unauthorized expeditions against Indians.

1677 **Culpeper's Rebellion**: Albemarle, Carolina, colonists imprison the deputy governor, convene a legislature, and run the government.

1689–1691 **Leisler's Rebellion**: Militia captain Jacob Leisler names himself governor of New York and tries to organize an expedition against French Canada.

1689–1697 **King William's War**: The French and Indians attack British in New York, New Hampshire, and Maine.

1702–1713 **Queen Anne's War**: French and Indians attack British settlements; British capture Acadia.

1711–1713 **Tuscarora War**: Tuscarora Indians attack settlers along North Carolina's Neuse and Pamlico rivers.

1715–1717 Yamasee War: Creek, Yamasee, Apalachee, Savannah, and Sarraw Indians attack South Carolina settlements.

1739–1742 War of Jenkins' Ear: England declares war on Spain as both nations try to expand their interests in America.

1744–1748 King George's War: French, Indians, and Spanish fight the British from French Canada to the Caribbean.

1754–1763 French and Indian War: British regulars and American colonials square off against the French and their Indian allies. The capture of Quebec ends French rule in Canada.

1758–1761 Cherokee Uprising: British and Cherokee fight in Tennessee, Virginia, and the Carolinas.

1763–1766 Pontiac's War: Pontiac leads the Ottawa, Wyandot, Potawatomi, and Ojibwa in an attempt to drive British settlers out of former French territories.

1763–1764 Paxton Boys Uprising: Pennsylvania frontiersmen march on Philadelphia and raid the Conestoga Indians.

1765–1766 Stamp Act Revolt: Sons of Liberty resist Britain's Stamp Act; it's repealed in March 1766.

1768–1771 Regulator War: Western North Carolina colonists fight government officials.

1770 Boston Massacre: British soldiers kill five Bostonians.

1773 Boston Tea Party: Colonists dressed as Indians board ships and dump tea into Boston Harbor.

1774 Lord Dunmore's War: Shawnee Indians fight Virginia settlers over colonists' expansion into the Appalachians.

1775–1783 American Revolution: Colonies fight for independence from Great Britain.

1786–1787 **Shays' Rebellion**: Suffering from a harsh economy, Massachusetts farmers march on Springfield; the state militia defeats the uprising.

1790–1812 **Ohio Valley campaigns**: US forces fight sporadic battles with Miami, Shawnee, and other tribes in what's now Ohio, Indiana, and Illinois.

1794 **Whiskey Rebellion**: Western Pennsylvanians protest the government's new tax on whiskey.

1798–1800 **Quasi-war with France**: French privateers prey on US merchant vessels, prompting an undeclared naval war between the United States and France.

1801–1805 **First Barbary War**: The United States attacks the Barbary state of Tripoli after refusing to pay tribute to pirates.

1812–1815 **War of 1812**: The United States takes on British forces, who burn Washington, DC.

1815 **Second Barbary War**: Algiers declares war on the United States.

1817–1818 **First Seminole War**: Conflict begins after US authorities try to reclaim runaway slaves living among the Seminole.

1832 **Black Hawk War**: Illinois and Wisconsin militia, supported by the US Army, take on the Sauk, Fox, Winnebago, Sioux, and Chippewa tribes.

1835–1842 **Second Seminole War**: War erupts after the Seminole Indians refuse to relocate west of the Mississippi River.

1836 **War of Texas Independence**: American settlers in Texas fight Mexico for independence.

1839–1846 **Anti-rent War**: New York farmers rebel against feudal landowner system.

1842 **Dorr Rebellion**: An attempt to reform Rhode Island's 1663 charter, under which only landowners can vote, becomes an armed uprising.

1846–1848 **Mexican War**: Mexico cedes what's now California, New Mexico, Arizona, Colorado, Utah, and Nevada to the United States.

1855–1858 **Third Seminole War**: The Seminole are defeated and moved from Florida.

1857–1858 **Utah War**: President Buchanan sends troops to enforce his appointment of non-Mormon governor Alfred Cumming.

1860–1900 **Plains and Western Indian wars**: Western states witness repeated conflicts between US settlers and American Indian inhabitants.

1861–1865 **Civil War**: Southern and Northern states fight over slavery and states' rights issues.

1864–1868 **Navajo wars**: After a series of treaties fails, Col. Kit Carson begins a scorched-earth policy that forces the Indians to surrender.

1866–1871 **The Fenian War**: The Irish-American movement launches five unsuccessful raids in Canada.

1898–1934 **The Banana Wars**: Marines quell revolts and stage military interventions in Haiti, the Dominican Republic, Nicaragua, Panama, and Cuba.

1898 **Spanish-American War**: The United States declares war on Spain and launches offensives in Cuba and the Philippines.

1899–1902 **Philippine Insurrection**: US troops clash with Filipino freedom fighters.

1900 **Boxer Rebellion**: The United States is part of an international force that ends a siege of Beijing.

1916–1917 Pancho Villa Expedition: US troops pursue the bandit and revolutionary Pancho Villa in Mexico.

1917–1918 World War I: More than 4 million Americans serve in the "The Great War."

1919–1920 Russian Civil War: The United States deploys to Vladivostok and Siberia to support anti–Bolshevik forces.

1941–1945 World War II: More than 16 million Americans fight in Europe, North Africa, and the Pacific.

1950–1953 Korean War: US troops, supported by the United Nations, help South Korea fight off invasions from North Korea in the first significant armed conflict of the Cold War.

1965–1973 Vietnam War: US troops aid South Vietnam against communist North Vietnam and its Viet Cong allies in this Cold War conflict.

War Records to Look For

Learn which military records to search for based on your ancestors' birth dates.

If your ancestor was born in...	Look for records of the...
1726–1767	Revolutionary War (1775–1783)
1762–1799	War of 1812 (1812–1815)
1796–1831	Mexican War (1846–1848)
1811–1848	Civil War (1861–1865)
1848–1881	Spanish–American War (1898)
1849–1885	Philippine Insurrection (1899–1902)
1872–1900	World War I (1917–1918)
1877–1925	World War II (1941–1945)
1900–1936	Korean War (1950–1953)
1914–1955	Vietnam War (early 1960s–1973)

Depending on the war in which your ancestor served, you'll find a variety of types of military records.

War	Service records/ Muster rolls	Pension records	Bounty land warrants	Draft cards
Colonial Wars	●		●	
Revolutionary War	●	●	●	
War of 1812	●	●	●	
Mexican War	●	●	●	
Civil War	●	●		
Spanish American War	●			
World War I	●			●
World War II	●			●
Korean War	●			
Vietnam War	●			

Military

US Military Record Sources

Check the repositories and websites listed for original military records on paper, on microfilm, or in digitized format. Large public, state, and university libraries also may have copies of National Archives and Records Administration (NARA) microfilm; search for books and websites with military record indexes and transcriptions, too.

Revolutionary War service records

- Ancestry.com (by subscription)
- Fold3 (by subscription)

Revolutionary War pension files

- Fold3
- HeritageQuest Online (available through subscribing libraries)
- NARA and Family History Library microfilm

Civil War service records

- Fold3
- NARA

Civil War US colored troops service records

- Ancestry.com
- NARA and Family History Library microfilm

Civil War pension index cards

- Ancestry.com: extends to 1934
- FamilySearch Record Search (index only)
- Fold3
- NARA and Family History Library microfilm

Civil War pensions

- NARA

Civil War widows' pension files

- Fold3

Mexican War service and pension records

- NARA

Spanish-American war service records

- NARA

WWI draft registration cards

- Ancestry.com
- NARA and Family History Library microfilm

WWI and later service records

- NARA (restricted for privacy reasons)

WWII draft registration cards

- Ancestry.com
- FamilySearch Record Search
- NARA and Family History Library microfilm

WWII enlistment database

- Ancestry.com
- Fold3
- NARA website

Rosters, muster rolls, militia records, adjutant general records, veterans surveys, correspondence, photos, battlefield maps, regimental histories

- State archives
- Military history organizations

10

CEMETERIES

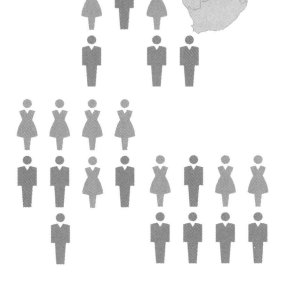

Tombstone Symbolism

ARCHITECTURAL

archway, **door**, or **gate** passageway into the next life

bench places of contemplation for mourners

broken pillar or **column** life cut short or sudden death

ANIMALS

bat death; misfortune

crane loyalty, vigilance

dove peace

lamb meekness, gentleness, innocence; God's flock
(popular on children's graves)

lion courage, strength, resurrection

phoenix resurrection

CLOTHING

helmet protection, faith

shoes—empty, **one overturned** loss of a child

FIGURES

angel dropping flowers on grave grief, mourning

angel pointing to heaven rejoicing

head with wings soul effigy indicating human mortality

naked baby or child new life, innocence, purity

FRUITS, NUTS, AND THE HARVEST

acorn strength, independence

fruit eternal plenty

pineapple welcome, perfection

wheat harvest, prosperity; deceased full of years

HANDS AND FINGERS

Cohanim hands (thumbs and forefingers touch) Judaism

forefinger pointing up soul has gone to heaven

hand reaching down God retrieving the deceased's soul

handshake God's welcome into heaven; marriage, if one hand is feminine and the other, masculine

INITIALS

AAONMS Ancient Arabic Order or Nobles and the Mystic Shrine (Masonic)

AASR Ancient and Accepted Scottish Rite (Masonic)

AOH Ancient Order of Hibernians

AOUW Ancient Order of United Workmen

BPOE Benevolent and Protective Order of Elks

FOE Fraternal Order of Eagles

G (with a compass and square) Masonic

IHC, HIS the first three letters of Jesus' name in Greek

IOOF Independent Order of Odd Fellows

K of C Knights of Columbus

WOW Woodmen of the World

MORTALITY

bone death

candle life

clock the march of time, usually stopped at the hour of death

skull, with crossbones or wings version of the winged death's head symbolizing the fleeting nature of life

OCCUPATIONS AND CRAFTS

church with a steeple minister

horses, two heads International Brotherhood of Teamsters, Chauffeurs, Warehousemen and Helpers of America

scales of justice lawyer

ship sailor or fisherman

ORNAMENTAL

basket maternal body, fertility

crook associated with Jesus as a shepherd
(often on the graves of Odd Fellows)

draped urn physical body; veil may refer to reverence or a veil between
earth and heaven

fountain the Virgin Mary

shield protection; faith; defense of the spirit

RELIGIOUS

cross Christianity

Star of David, menorah, Levite pitcher, Cohanim hands
(see Hands and Fingers) Judaism

TREES, PLANTS AND FLOWERS

daisy simplicity, the Virgin Mary (often on the graves of children)

fern humility, sincerity

lily purity

morning glory resurrection

oak leaf strength of faith

olive tree or branch reconciliation between God and man; peace

thistle Scottish heritage

tree stump life cut short (often on graves of members of
Woodmen of the World)

vine relationship between God and man

weeping willow, sometimes with urn sorrow

wheat long, fruitful life

Cemeteries

Cemetery Do's and Don'ts

Do ...

★ Bring a camera, reflective surface (such as foil-covered cardboard), notebook, pens, carpenter's apron, gardener's knee pads, garden shears, whisk broom, sunscreen, and moist towelettes.

★ Wear protective clothing and boots and carry bug repellent.

★ Take personal safety precautions, such as bringing a friend and carrying your cell phone.

★ Watch for uneven ground, since graves tend to sink.

★ Notice who's buried around your ancestor—they could be relatives.

★ Note the exact location in relationship to the cemetery entrance (record the GPS coordinates if you have a device) and mark it on a cemetery map.

★ Take pictures of the tombstone with a variety of lighting and angles. Also photograph the grounds and graveyard entrance.

★ Note the type of stone that marks your ancestor's grave and any artwork on the stone.

★ Write down the full inscription on the stone.

★ Leave flowers with your contact information attached on or shortly before Memorial Day or the town's decoration day—a distant cousin might show up to pay respects.

Don't ...

✖ Just rush to find your ancestor's grave, photograph the tombstone, and leave.

✖ Visit when it's getting dark, or go alone to an isolated cemetery.

✖ Cross private land to get to a cemetery, unless you get the landowner's permission first.

✖ Clean or otherwise touch any tombstones, including creating tombstone rubbings.

✖ Use acidic compounds such as vinegar or shaving cream on tombstones—they can eat away at the stone.

✖ Interfere with anyone paying respects or attending funerals.

Tombstone Materials Timeline

1650s and earlier: fieldstones, boulders, and wood markers

1660s–1850s: sandstone, limestone, and slate

1830s–1880s: marble

1880s–1910s: soft, gray granite, and cast metal

1920s-present: granite

Types of Cemeteries

church/religious May be adjacent to a church or other religious organization's building; especially common in New England and the Southeast.

ethnic A cemetery where those of a particular ethnicity were historically buried. May also be a religious or other type of cemetery.

family or **private** Small plots with graves of local families often in a rural setting; usually maintained by the town or county government or a local historical society.

garden Beautifully landscaped with trees, flowers, fountains, and paths winding around monuments and tombstones; popular starting in the 1800s.

memorial park Landscaped lawns and gardens with flat, ground-level plaques marking graves; introduced in the early 1900s.

potter's fields Public cemeteries where the poor and unclaimed bodies often were buried.

veterans cemeteries Nationally, state-, or locally owned military cemeteries where veterans and their families may be buried.

Cemeteries

4 Cemetery Search Tips

1. **Find the burial place**. Try to learn where your ancestor is buried from funeral cards, death certificates, obituaries, or other family papers. If these sources list a funeral home, check the *American Blue Book of Funeral Service* (Kates-Boylston Publications, 1932) for contact information. If the home no longer exists, run a Google **<www.google. com>** search to see if another home bought it, and check local or state historical societies for information on what happened to its records.

2. **Look for published tombstone transcriptions**. Before you travel to a distant cemetery, look for a published transcription. Search the Family History Library's (FHL) online catalog **<www.familysearch.org>** on the place name, then look for a cemetery category in your results. On many websites (see Cemetery Research Resources), you can search volunteer-submitted tombstone transcriptions and photographs.

3. **Get burial records**. Many transcriptions are online, posted by fellow genealogists, cemeteries or government agencies. Search the sites in the next section. If the record isn't online, write to the cemetery sexton if the cemetery is still active. For inactive cemeteries, write to the town hall or county courthouse where the cemetery is located.

4. **Check vital stats**. Some tombstone markers offer just a name and death date. More-elaborate stones may give the date of birth, places of birth and death, age at death, parents' and spouse's names, and a verse (called the epitaph). You may see a person's age written this way: *Died March 25, 1846, aged 37 years, 3 months and 15 days*. To determine the birth date, you can use an online calculator such as the one at **<www.longislandgenealogy.com/birth.html>**.

Cemetery Research Resources

The A to Z of Tombstone Art <www.tales.co.uk/index-atozart.html>

American Battle Monuments Commission <www.abmc.gov>

Association for Gravestone Studies <www.gravestonestudies.org>

BillionGraves <www.billiongraves.com>

Cemetery Symbolism: A Wary Glossary
<www.alsirat.com/symbols/symbols1.html>

Cyndi's List: Cemeteries <www.cyndislist.com/cemeteries>

Find A Grave <www.findagrave.com>

Genealogy.com Virtual Cemetery
<www.genealogy.com/vcem_welcome.html>

Interment.net <www.interment.net>

Names in Stone <www.namesinstone.com>

Nationwide Gravesite Locator <gravelocator.cem.va.gov>

Obituary Central <www.obitcentral.com>

Saving Graves <www.savinggraves.net>

USGenWeb Tombstone Transcription Project
<www.usgwtombstones.org>

USGS Geographic Names Information System <geonames.usgs.gov>
Select Cemetery from the Feature Class list when you search for known
cemeteries in the area.

TheCemeteryClub <www.thecemeteryclub.com>

Cemeteries

The American Resting Place: 400 Years of History Through Our Cemeteries and Burial Grounds by Marilyn Yalom (Houghton Mifflin Harcourt, 2008)

Cemeteries of the US: A Guide to Contact Information for US Cemeteries and Their Records by Deborah M. Burek (Gale Group, 1994)

Corpses, Coffins, and Crypts: A History of Burial by Penny Colman (Square Fish, 2015)

The Family Tree Cemetery Field Guide by Joy Neighbors (Family Tree Books, 2017)

Stories in Stone: The Complete Guide to Cemetery Symbolism by Douglas Keister (Gibbs Smith, 2004)

Stories Told in Stone: Cemetery Iconography by Gaylord Cooper (MOTES, 2009)

3 Steps to Photograph a Tombstone

STEP 1 BRING THE RIGHT TOOLS

To take a photograph of a tombstone, you'll need:
- camera and memory card (or film), plus extra batteries
- spray bottle filled with water
- plastic or nylon brush (never wire)
- rags
- mirror (preferably full-length) or foil-covered cardboard

STEP 2 PREP THE TOMBSTONE

If the stone is sturdy and in good shape, lightly clean it by spraying it with water and gently removing debris with your brush and rag.

If the stone is crumbling or unsteady, don't touch it. Wet the stone to bring out the transcription (avoid any other substances such as chalk or shaving cream).

STEP 3 GET GOOD LIGHTING

Photographs turn out better when taken in early morning light. In many cemeteries, graves lie on an east-west axis, and late afternoon light may cast your shadow on west-facing inscriptions. Use a mirror or foil to reflect light onto the stone for a better photograph (bring along an assistant to hold the reflector).

Cemeteries

11

GENETIC GENEALOGY

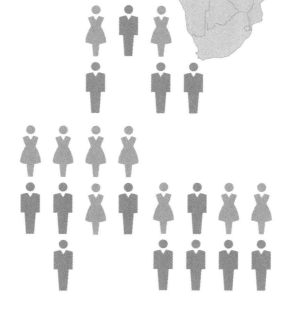

Genetic Genealogy
Testing Companies

23andMe <www.23andme.com>

African Ancestry <www.africanancestry.com>

AncestryDNA <dna.ancestry.com>

DNA Consultants <dnaconsultants.com>

Family Tree DNA <www.familytreedna.com>

Living DNA <www.livingdna.com>

MyHeritage DNA <www.myheritage.com/dna>

National Geographic Genographic Project
<genographic.nationalgeographic.com>

Oxford Ancestors <www.oxfordancestors.com>

Pathway Genomics <www.pathway.com>

Genetic Genealogy

DNA Analysis Tools

DNAGedcom <www.dnagedcom.com>
This heavy-duty tool provides reams of useful data on genetic relatives, perfect for triangulation.

DNALand <dna.land>
Use this tool to analyze ethnicity estimates and find genetic cousins.

GEDmatch <www.gedmatch.com>
This tool, arguably the most popular, allows you to run more-detailed DNA reports and compare DNA results across testing companies.

Genetic Genealogy Tools <www.y-str.org>
Among this site's analysis tools are an X-DNA Relationship Path Finder and an Autosomal Segment Analyzer.

Genome Mate Pro <www.getgmp.com>
This tool compiles data from multiple sources into a single file, then runs triangulation and chromosome mapping.

Kitty Munson Cooper's Segment Mapper
<www.kittymunson.com/dna/SegmentMapper.php>
This free tool generates a chromosome-style chart.

Types of DNA Tests

	mtDNA	Y-DNA	atDNA	X-DNA
Types of testing	**HVR1/HVR2 sequencing:** Testing regions of DNA that are more likely to change **Whole-mtDNA sequencing:** Testing the full mtDNA strand **SNP testing:** Testing specific DNA sites	**Y-STR testing:** Testing short repeated segments of DNA **Y-SNP testing:** Testing specific DNA sites	**SNP testing:** Testing specific DNA sites **Whole-genome sequencing:** Testing all twenty-three chromosomes	(SNP testing is part of an atDNA test)
Haplogroup determination?	Yes	Yes. Y-DNA test results are used to either estimate (for Y-STR test) or determine (for Y-SNP testing) the test-taker's paternal haplogroup.	No	No
Cousin matching?	Yes. HVR1/HVR2 and whole-mtDNA sequencing can be used for cousin matching, although random matches may not be meaningful in a genealogically relevant timescale since mtDNA mutates slowly. SNP testing is not used for cousin matching.	Yes. Y-STR test results are useful for random cousin matching for estimating the number of paternal generations between two matches. Y-SNP testing is not as useful.	Yes. atDNA test results are useful for random cousin matching and for roughly estimating the number of generations between two matches.	Yes, although (due to low SNP density and low thresholds) only large segments should be considered (at least 10 cMs, and possibly larger)

Genetic Genealogy

Comparing Autosomal DNA Tests at a Glance

		23andMe	Ancestry DNA	Family Tree DNA	MyHeritage DNA
General Information	regular price (check for discounts)	$99	$99	$99	$79
	database size	more than 5 million	more than 10 million	nearly 1 million (atDNA, Y-DNA, and mtDNA)	more than 1 million
	subscription required	no	yes, for most analysis tools	no	yes, for most analysis tools
	accessiblity to customer service	e-mail only	phone, e-mail	phone, e-mail	phone, e-mail
	contact your match	via e-mail brokering	via e-mail brokering	e-mail directly	e-mail brokering
	ethnic population groups	150	150	24	42
Genealogy Tools	quality of pedigree viewer	poor	excellent	OK	OK
	search matches by surname and location	yes	yes	yes	yes
	integrate pedigree with DNA	no (customers can provide basic family information)	yes	no (customers can provide a GEDCOM and basic family information)	yes
	specific relationship suggested	yes	yes	no	yes
	amount of shared DNA (in cM)	yes	no	yes	yes
	chromosome browser	yes	no	yes	yes

DNA Relationship Comparison Chart

Average shared cM*	Average percentage of shared DNA**	Relationship	Range of shared cM***
3,400	50%	Parent/child	3,330-3,720
2,550	50%	Full sibling	2,209-3,384
1,700	25%	Half sibling	1,317-2,312
		Aunt/uncle/niece/nephew	1,349-2,175
		Double first cousin	2,209-3,384
		Grandparent/grandchild	1,156-2,311
850	12.5%	First cousin	553-1,225
		Half-aunt/half-uncle/half-niece/half-nephew	500-1,446
		Great-grandparent/great-grandchild	464-1,486
		Great-aunt/great-uncle/great-niece/great-nephew	251-2,108
425	6.25%	First cousin once removed	141-851
		Half-first cousin	137-856
		Half-great-aunt/half-great-uncle/half-great-niece/half-great-nephew	125-765
212.5	3.125%	Second cousin	46-515
		First cousin twice removed	43-531
		Half-first cousin once removed	57-530
106.25	1.56%	Second cousin once removed	0-316
		Half-second cousin	9-397
		First cousin three times removed	0-283
		Half-first cousin twice removed	37-360
53.13	0.78%	Third cousin	0-217
		Second cousin twice removed	0-261
26.56	0.391%	Third cousin once removed	0-173

*AncestryDNA, MyHeritage DNA, and Family Tree DNA provide shared DNA in centimorgans (cM).
**23andMe provides shared DNA as a percentage.
***According to the shared cM Project, a study of cMs shared by known relatives. For more information, see <thegeneticgenealogist.com/2017/08/26/august-2017-update-to-the-shared-cm-project>.

Genetic Genealogy

5 Genetic Genealogy Myths

Myth: Geneticists use hair and blood samples to trace a person's ancestry.
Reality: Genetic genealogy tests usually involve swishing mouthwash or taking a cheek swab.

Myth: A DNA test can pinpoint precisely where your ancestors lived or which tribe they belonged to.
Reality: Human migration throughout history makes pinpointing ancestral locations or tribes extremely difficult. Combining genetic genealogy with traditional research, though, can help you discover ancestral origins.

Myth: To find out if you and another researcher descend from the same third-great-grandfather, you need to dig up his body for a DNA sample to test.
Reality: Find a descendant of your third-great-grandfather through a male line, and ask him to take a test. This man would have inherited Great-great-great-grandpa's Y-DNA.

Myth: The results of ancestral DNA tests are 99.9 percent accurate, just like the DNA tests on *CSI*.
Reality: Genetic genealogy involves a lot of analysis and interpretation. DNA test results are presented in terms of probabilities. In most cases, they can suggest—but not prove—relationships.

Myth: If you take a DNA test, you can finally find out who your great-grandmother's parents were.
Reality: A DNA test can't identify who your ancestors were. It can only indicate with whom you share DNA.

Genetic Genealogy Resources

23andMe Blog <blog.23andme.com>

AncestryDNA Blog <blogs.ancestry.com/ancestry/category/dna>

Cyndi's List: Genetics, DNA, and Family Health
<www.cyndislist.com/dna>

Cyndi's List: Surname DNA Studies and Projects
<www.cyndislist.com/surnames/dna>

DNAeXplained—Genetic Genealogy by Roberta Estes
<dna-explained.com>

Genealem's Genetic Genealogy
<genealem-geneticgenealogy.blogspot.com>

Genetealogy <www.genetealogy.com>

The Genetic Genealogist by Blaine T. Bettinger
<www.thegeneticgenealogist.com>

International Society of Genetic Genealogy <isogg.org>

Journal of Genetic Genealogy <www.jogg.info>

Kitty Cooper's Blog: Musing on Genealogy, Genetics, and Gardening
<blog.kittycooper.com>

Segment-ology <www.segmentology.org>

Through the Trees <throughthetreesblog.tumblr.com>

Your DNA Guide by Diahan Southard <www.yourdnaguide.com>

Your Genetic Genealogist by CeCe Moore
<www.yourgeneticgenealogist.com>

Genetic Genealogy

The Adoptee's Guide to DNA Testing by Tamar Weinberg (Family Tree Books, 2018)

Deep Ancestry: Inside The Genographic Project by Spencer Wells (National Geographic, 2007)

DNA & Genealogy by Colleen Fitzpatrick (Rice Book Press, 2005)

DNA and Tradition: The Genetic Link to the Ancient Hebrews by Yaakov Kleiman (Devora Publishing, 2004)

The Family Tree Guide to DNA Testing and Genetic Genealogy by Blaine T. Bettinger (Family Tree Books, 2016)

Genetic Genealogy: The Basics and Beyond by Emily D. Aulicino (AuthorHouse, 2013)

Genetic Genealogy in Practice by Blaine T. Bettinger and Debbie Parker Wayne (National Genealogical Society, 2016)

Saxons, Vikings, and Celts: The Genetic Roots of Britain and Ireland by Bryan Sykes (W.W. Norton & Co., 2007)

The Seven Daughters of Eve by Bryan Sykes (W.W. Norton & Co.)

Trace Your Roots With DNA by Megan Smolenyak Smolenyak and Ann Turner (Rodale, 2004)

12

GEOGRAPHY

Rectangular Survey System

SECTIONS IN A TOWNSHIP

					640 acres
6	5	4	3	2	1
7	8	9	10	11	12
13	14	15	16	17	18
19	20	21	22	23	24
30	29	28	27	26	25
31	32	33	34	35	36

6 miles (vertical) · 6 miles (horizontal)

Public-land states divvied up parcels of property according to the rectangular survey system. The principal meridian—an imaginary north-south line—serves as the starting point for surveying a 24×24-mile tract. A tract is divided into 16 townships; every township (23,040 acres) contains 36 sections, each 1 square mile (640 acres).

DIVISIONS OF A SECTION

40 acres NW ¼ NW ¼	NE ¼ NW ¼	**160 acres** NE ¼ Section
SW ¼ NW ¼	SE ¼ NW¼	
80 acres N ½ SW ¼	**80 acres** W ½ SE ¼	E ½ SW ¼
S ½ SW ¼		

1 mile (vertical) — 1 mile (horizontal)

A section could be split into halves, quarters or otherwise. The descriptions of those subdivisions (such as "the north half of the southwest quarter," or N½ SW¼ for short) are called aliquot parts.

US Territorial Acquisitions Timeline

1783 Former British colonies

1803 Louisiana Purchase (828,800 square miles in what's now Arkansas, Missouri, Iowa, Oklahoma, Kansas, Nebraska, part of Minnesota, most of North Dakota and South Dakota, northeastern New Mexico, parts of Montana, Wyoming, and Colorado; and Louisiana west of the Mississippi River)

1819 Florida

1845 Texas

1846 Oregon Territory

1848 Mexican Cession (California, Nevada, and Utah, plus parts of Colorado, New Mexico, Arizona, and Wyoming)

1853 Gadsden Purchase (a strip of southern Arizona and New Mexico)

1867 Alaska, Midway Islands

1898 Hawaiian islands, Philippine islands, Guam, Puerto Rico

1899 American Samoa

1903 Panama Canal Zone

1917 Virgin Islands

US Territorial Acquisitions Map

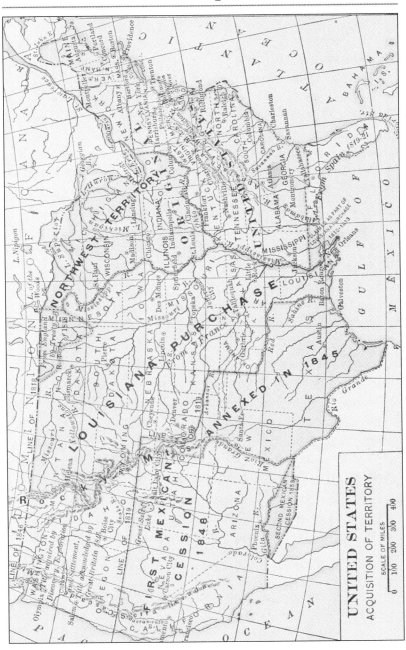

UNITED STATES
ACQUISITION OF TERRITORY

SCALE OF MILES
0 100 200 300 400

Major US Population Migrations

LATE-1700S–1800S

As the United States grew, made treaties with Indians, and awarded land bounties for Revolutionary War and War of 1812 service, settlers migrated from the original states to the Old Southwest (Alabama and Mississippi), the Old Northwest (Ohio, Indiana, Illinois, Michigan, Wisconsin, and northeastern Minnesota), Kentucky, and Tennessee.

1848–1855

The discovery of gold at Sutter's Mill in Coloma, California, touched off the California Gold Rush; an estimated 300,000 Americans and immigrants hurried to California.

1862–1934

The Homestead Act encouraged Americans to move to unoccupied land in the West. Eventually, 1.6 million homesteads were granted on 270 million acres of federal land.

POST-RECONSTRUCTION

Racial oppression led many freedmen to leave the South. African-American migrants to Kansas in 1879 and 1880 became known as Exodusters.

LATE 1800S-EARLY 1900S

As the United States industrialized, towns and cities (mostly in the North) swelled with migrants from farms who went to work in mills, factories, and offices.

1930–1940

By 1940, the severe dust storms of the Dust Bowl had caused 2.5 million people to flee the Plains states; 200,000 of them to California.

1910–1940

The Great Migration saw 1.75 million African-Americans leave the rural South for cities in the North and Midwest, such as New York, Baltimore, Philadelphia, Chicago, Detroit, and St. Louis.

1940–1970

More than 5 million African-Americans moved from the South to cities in the North, Midwest, and West.

Major US Migration Routes

BRADDOCK'S ROAD: NEW YORK, AND PENNSYLVANIA
This route connected Cumberland, Maryland, on the Potomac River to the Monongahela River south of present-day Pittsburgh. In 1813, construction began on the Cumberland Road (later, the National Road), which followed much the same route.

CALIFORNIA TRAIL: UTAH, CALIFORNIA, OREGON, AND WASHINGTON
Blazed in 1841, this trail split off of the Oregon Trail at Soda Springs, Idaho, after Fort Bridger. It followed the Bear River and crossed the Great Salt Lake Desert and Sierra Nevadas.

California Gold Rush migrants tried other routes. Some went north of the Great Salt Lake and through a corner of Idaho to rejoin the trail at the Humboldt River. From Nevada, the Lassen Route aimed north of Sutter's Mill, while the southerly Carson Route headed southwest.

CAROLINA ROAD: VIRGINIA, THE CAROLINAS, AND GEORGIA
An alternative to the Fall Line Road, the Carolina Road (also called the Upper Road) tracked through Hillsboro and Charlotte, North Carolina, in the 1750s. It originally extended to Greenville, South Carolina, but in 1828 connected to the Federal Road at Athens, Georgia.

CHICAGO ROAD: NORTHWEST TERRITORY
This crude road from Detroit to Chicago, built between 1829 and 1836, brought pioneers to southern Michigan and Illinois.

DE ANZA TRAIL: ARIZONA, UTAH, CALIFORNIA, OREGON, WASHINGTON
In 1776, Spanish Lt. Col. Juan Bautista de Anza led almost three hundred people over 1,200 miles to settle Alta (Upper) California. The first overland route connecting New Spain with San Francisco, the US segment begins at Nogales, Arizona.

EL CAMINO REAL DE LOS TEJAS: SOUTHWEST
During the Spanish colonial period, this was the primary overland trail from what's now Mexico, across the Rio Grande to east Texas and the Red River Valley in what's now northwest Louisiana.

EL CAMINO REAL DE TIERRA ADENTRO: SOUTHWEST

This north-south route connected Mexico City with what's now northern New Mexico. Its US section stretches from El Paso, Texas, to San Juan Pueblo, New Mexico.

FALL LINE ROAD: VIRGINIA, THE CAROLINAS, AND GEORGIA

Beginning in about 1735, travelers would leave King's Highway at Fredericksburg, Virginia, and head southwest to Augusta, Georgia, at the head of the Savannah River. Eventually, many Alabama- and Mississippi-bound pioneers would follow the Fall Line Road to link up with the new Federal Road in Columbus, Georgia.

FEDERAL ROAD: ALABAMA, MISSISSIPPI, LOUISIANA, AND TEXAS

In 1806, Congress appropriated $6,400 for this road to carry mail between Athens, Georgia, and New Orleans. It was widened and partly rerouted in 1811; connecting Fort Stoddert, Alabama (north of Mobile), to Fort Wilkinson, Georgia, on the Chattahoochee River, where the route merged with the original postal path.

GREAT VALLEY ROAD: VIRGINIA, THE CAROLINAS, AND GEORGIA

Known to Indians as the Great Warrior Path, this trail's forerunner reached from New York to present-day Salisbury, North Carolina, where it connected with the Great Trading Path.

Its feeders included the Philadelphia Wagon Road, which in the 1740s, linked up with the Pioneer's Road from Alexandria, Virginia, and went on to Winchester, Virginia. The Great Valley Road also became a feeder into the Wilderness Road.

KING'S HIGHWAY: VIRGINIA, THE CAROLINAS, AND GEORGIA

Incorporating the Boston Post Road between Boston and New York, King's Highway could be called America's first interstate. It eventually stretched 1,300 miles south from Boston through most of the Colonies' important cities, to Charleston, South Carolina.

MOHAWK TRAIL: NEW YORK AND PENNSYLVANIA

By 1770, this trail reached from Albany to Buffalo. The Catskill Turnpike overlapped it after the Revolutionary War. In 1825, the Erie Canal provided a waterway from Albany, New York, to Lake Erie.

MORMON TRAIL: UTAH, CALIFORNIA, OREGON, AND WASHINGTON

Mormon leader Brigham Young set off with his followers from Nauvoo, Illinois, in 1846. They crossed Iowa and the Missouri River to the site of present-day Florence, Nebraska, then traced the north bank of the Platte River from Fort Kearny, Nebraska, to Fort Laramie, Wyoming, where they turned southwest to Salt Lake City, Utah.

NATCHEZ TRACE: TENNESSEE, MISSISSIPPI, AND LOUISIANA

The first major north-south route in the South, the Natchez Trace followed Indian trails from Nashville, Tennessee, to Natchez, Mississippi, on the Mississippi River. The 500-mile route was upgraded in 1806, and briefly supplanted by the Jackson Military Road, which reached New Orleans in 1820.

NATIONAL ROAD: NORTHWEST TERRITORY

Originally the Cumberland Road, the route was called the National Road by 1825 because of its Congressional funding. Construction of the 600-mile span, which eventually stretched from Cumberland, Maryland, (incorporating the old Braddock's Road) to Vandalia, Illinois, began in 1811.

OLD SPANISH TRAIL: SOUTHWEST

This trail and its variants connected Los Angeles and Santa Fe, New Mexico, (key outposts of what was then Mexico) from 1829 to 1848. The 2,700-mile trail crossed deserts, canyons, and Death Valley.

OREGON TRAIL: UTAH, CALIFORNIA, OREGON, AND WASHINGTON

The Oregon Trail covered two thousand miles in seven states. It stretched from Independence, Missouri, to Fort Kearny in Nebraska, followed the south bank of the Platte River, crossed Wyoming to Fort Bridger, then turned northwest through what's now Idaho. At The Dalles, Oregon, migrants took the Columbia River or (after 1846) the safer but longer Barlow toll road across the Cascade Range to the Willamette Valley.

PENNSYLVANIA ROAD: NEW YORK AND PENNSYLVANIA

Incorporating the Great Conestoga Road and then later Lancaster Pike, the Pennsylvania Road connected Philadelphia to Pittsburgh. Much of the route west of Harrisburg, Pennsylvania, followed the early path of Forbes Road.

RICHMOND ROAD: KENTUCKY AND TENNESSEE

Many settlers bound for Kentucky traveled this route through Virginia from Richmond to Fort Chiswell, where it joined the Great Valley Road.

Geography

SANTA FE TRAIL: SOUTHWEST

More a commercial route than a migration path, this famous trail also was traveled by gold seekers and by American troops in the war with Mexico from 1821 until the railroad arrived in 1880. The 1,200-mile route crossed five states, from Franklin, Missouri, to Santa Fe, New Mexico.

STATE ROAD: NORTHWEST TERRITORY

Connecting to the Chicago Road, the State Road extended west from Chicago through Elgin and Rockford to Galena, Illinois, on the Mississippi River.

WILDERNESS ROAD: KENTUCKY AND TENNESSEE

Daniel Boone led six families through the Cumberland Gap into Kentucky in 1775, pathfinding what was originally called Boone's Trace but would become known as the Wilderness Road when it was widened in 1796. Tennessee-bound settlers took the Knoxville Road south from Kentucky to the Nashville Road, or the Nickajack Trail from Fort Loudon (now in Tennessee) to the Chickasaw Trail (later renamed Robert's Road).

ZANE'S TRACE: NORTHWEST TERRITORY

In 1796 and 1797, Col. Ebenezer Zane built this road through Ohio between Wheeling, West Virginia, and Maysville, Kentucky. The segment between Wheeling and Zanesville, Ohio, also called the Wheeling Road, was ultimately upgraded and incorporated into the National Road.

10 Online Mapping Resources

Bureau of Land Management General Land Office Records
<glorecords.blm.gov/default.aspx>
Besides federal land title records for Eastern public-land states, researchers can find the original surveyors' field notes, survey plats, master title plats, and images of land warrants issued as a reward for military service.

eHistory <ehistory.osu.edu>
With hundreds of searchable historical maps, this site is strongest on the Civil War.

Getty Thesaurus of Geographic Names Online
<www.getty.edu/research/tools/vocabularies/index.html>
This database of more than 1.1 million locales includes current and historical spots around the world.

Google Earth <www.google.com/earth>
"Fly" across the planet to view satellite imagery, maps, terrain, 3-D buildings, and historical imagery.

Historic Map Works
<www.proquest.com/products-services/hmw.html>
ProQuest's collection (available through subscribing libraries) features more than 200,000 maps including property maps back to the late 1700s and antiquarian maps from the fifteenth to nineteenth centuries.

JewishGen ShtetlSeeker <www.jewishgen.org/communities>
Results in this database of localities in Central and Eastern Europe, the former Soviet Republics and Turkey link to historical names, maps, and more.

Library of Congress American Memory Collection
<memory.loc.gov/ammem/browse/updatedList.html>
Digitized maps here detail the Revolutionary Era, Louisiana Purchase, Civil War, World War II, railroads, US and Canadian cities, and more.

Perry-Castañeda Map Collection <www.lib.utexas.edu/maps>
Find historical maps from around the world in this vast collection from the University of Texas library.

UK Ordnance Survey

<www.ordnancesurvey.co.uk/shop>

Search for small-scale, high-detail maps of anywhere in the United Kingdom, then purchase.

US Geological Survey <store.usgs.gov>

Buy or download current maps, topographic maps back to 1882, and aerial maps. You also can look up places in the National Atlas or Geographic Names Information System.

4 Key Types of Maps

ENUMERATION DISTRICT MAPS

Created: To organize enumeration efforts during the US census

Notes: These maps indicate how a region was divided for census purposes in a given year. Large numbers indicate the enumeration district (ED). Find your ancestor's ED on the map, then browse census records for hard-to-find families. You can find ED maps for 1900 to 1940 at FamilySearch.org **<www.familysearch.org>**.

Research uses

- Finding ancestors hiding in the census
- Tracking communities over time

Higher-population areas require more EDs, and so you may need to consult an inset (such as here, where EDs 2-21 through 2-56 are on a separate map).

ED numbers are typically handwritten and larger than other digits you might see, such as ward numbers or sections of a township.

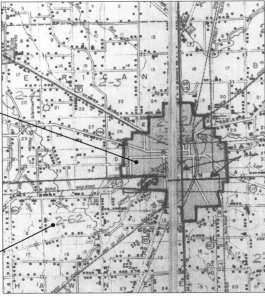

Source: National Archives and Records Administration

MILITARY MAPS

Created: To make strategic military decisions during conflicts; to track and document units' movements

Notes: Military maps can show individual regiment movements, defense garrisons, and the locations of important strategic events. Look to the key for information about what the different colors and textures indicate.

Research uses

- Tracing ancestors' regiments
- Understanding military records
- Studying historical battles

> Look for a key that may identify individual units or commanders.

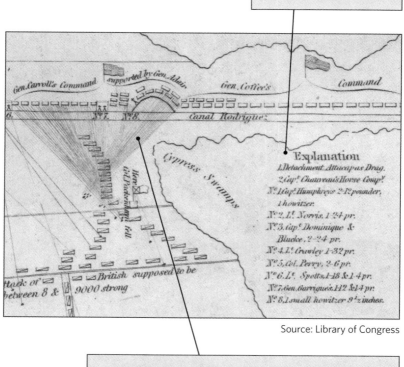

Source: Library of Congress

> Maps sometimes provide clues to each combatant's strategic advantage. These lines represent sight-lines for the Americans defending artillery and sharpshooters, who proved pivotal.

PLAT MAPS

Created: To track land ownership

Notes: Governments created plat maps (also called cadastral maps or survey plats) to account for parcels of land. The numbers indicate administrative divisions, and maps usually also include landowners' names. These maps weren't kept as consistently as ED or Sanborn maps. Look for them at state archives and digitized online (search for a town, county, or township at the Library of Congress or David Rumsey Map Collection website).

Research uses

- Locating your ancestor's land
- Finding land records
- Learning about communities
- Understanding town histories

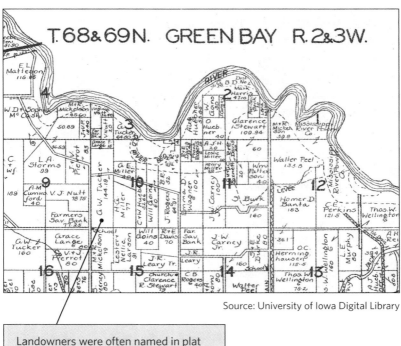

Source: University of Iowa Digital Library

Landowners were often named in plat maps. Use these details to find land and property records, such as deeds.

SANBORN MAPS

Created: To assess buildings' fire risk for insurance purposes.

Notes: Sanborn maps are perhaps the most consistent and widely available geographical record, providing detailed information about towns and cities across the United States. Unlike other kinds of maps, Sanborn maps have a fairly standardized key (see an example below). The Library of Congress has a large, free collection of Sanborn maps on its website <www.loc.gov/collections/sanborn-maps>.

Research uses

- Finding land and property records
- Tracking ancestors' addresses
- Understanding a town's social history

Buildings are colored to indicate the building material (stone, brick, iron, etc.). Notes show the structure's function.

Sanborn maps often list the names of individual buildings, a huge boon for those looking for property records.

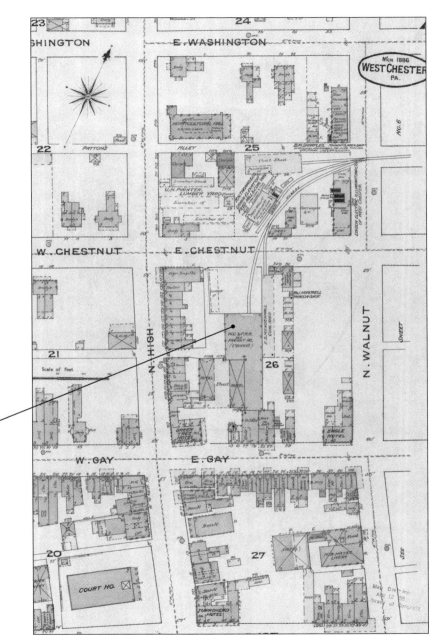

Source: Library of Congress

13

SOCIAL HISTORY

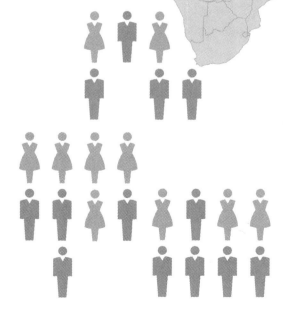

Timeline of Inventions

1596 Galileo invents the thermoscope.

1616 Castile soap is first made in Spain from olive oil.

1673 Johannes Hevelius builds a 140-foot-long refracting telescope.

1747 Andreas Marggraf extracts sugar from beets.

1765 Scotsman James Watt develops an improved version of Thomas Newcomen's steam engine.

1778 Scotsman Andrew Meikle invents the threshing machine.

1783 In France, the Marquis de Jouffroy d'Abbans steams a small boat, the *Pyroscaphe*, across the Seine.

1784 A baker from Gouda makes the first Belgian waffle.

1793 Eli Whitney invents the cotton gin.

1796 Edward Jenner tests the first smallpox vaccine.

1807 The first steamship, the *Clermont*, travels 150 miles from New York City to Albany in 32 hours.

1810 Vermont engraver James Wilson makes the first American globes for classroom use.

1819 France issues the first roller-skate patent.

1823 Samuel Read Hall receives a patent for a blackboard.

1838 British and American Steam Navigation Co.'s *Sirius* crosses the Atlantic entirely on steam power.

1843 The first Christmas card is designed by Englishman J.C. Horsley.

1844 Samuel Morse demonstrates his telegraph messaging system, sending a message from the Whig Party convention in Baltimore to the Capitol Building in Washington, DC.

1846 Belgian Adolphe Sax invents the saxophone.

1853 Potato chips are invented in Saratoga Springs, New York.

1857 Elisha Graves Otis installs the first commercial passenger elevator.

1858 The first working trans-Atlantic telegraph cable lasts only a month.

1858 Heinrich Geissler perfects the glass tube vacuum.

1866 Jack Daniel starts making whiskey in Lynchburg, Tennessee.

1876 Thomas Edison patents the mimeograph.

1879 Constantin Fahlberg and Ira Remsen accidentally discover saccharin.

1882 Schuyler Skaats Wheele invents the electric fan.

1883 Jan E. Matzeliger patents a shoe-lasting machine that cuts the price of shoes in half.

1884 Lewis Waterman patents the first practical fountain pen.

1888 George Eastman sells cameras to amateurs with the slogan "You push the button, we do the rest."

1892 Lever voting machines are first used in Lockport, New York.

1893 Charles and Frank Duryea convert a horse-drawn buggy to a gasoline-powered car.

1903 Orville and Wilbur Wright's *Flyer* sails 120 feet through the air in 12 seconds.

1904 D. McFarland Moore installs the first glowing-gas sign.

1907 Leo Baekeland creates Bakelite, the first completely synthetic manmade substance.

1907 The first photocopier, the rectigraph, is invented.

1908 Ford introduces the Model T; Melitta Bentz invents the drip coffeemaker.

1910 Georges Claude displays the first neon light sign in Paris.

1933 The first drive-in movie theater opens in Camden, New Jersey.

1935 Beer is first sold in cans.

1938 Chester Carlson makes his first electrophotographic image (a precursor to the copy machine).

1938 Berlin, New Hampshire, native Earl Tupper invents Tupperware.

1945 The first widespread influenza vaccine is released.

1956 The first trans-Atlantic telephone cable is laid.

1959 Coors develops the aluminum beverage can.

Timeline of Disasters

1747–1748 Record snowfalls in much of the United States.

1780 A hurricane hits the Caribbean, destroying British and French fleets and killing an estimated 22,000.

1815 The Great September Gale is the first hurricane to strike New England in 180 years.

1816 Crops fail during an unseasonably cool summer in New England, called the "The Year Without a Summer," after ash from a volcanic eruption in Indonesia causes a worldwide climate shift.

1845 Rain in Ireland exacerbates the Great Potato Famine and encourages emigration.

1853 The first major US rail disaster kills forty-six at Norwalk, Connecticut.

1868–1869 Great Lakes storms sink or run aground more than 3,000 ships, killing 500-plus people

1869 A coal mine disaster kills 110 people in Avondale, Pennsylvania.

1871 Hundreds die in the Great Chicago Fire; other fires rage in Michigan and Peshtigo, Wisconsin.

1873 The US Army Signal Corps issues its first hurricane warning.

1873–1877 Swarms of locusts damage $200 million in crops in Colorado, Minnesota, Nebraska, Wyoming, and elsewhere.

1876 A train wreck near Ashtabula, Ohio, claims 83 lives.

1881 A hurricane hits Georgia and the Carolinas, killing 700.

1884 On February 19, tornadoes kill hundreds in southeastern states.

1888 A January blizzard kills hundreds in Montana, Dakota Territory, and Nebraska; 400 die in the Northeast during the Great Blizzard.

1889 Heavy rains collapse a dam at Johnstown, Pennsylvania, killing more than 2,000.

1898 An avalanche near Sheep Camp, Alaska, is the deadliest event of the Klondike Gold Rush.

1900 A hurricane in Galveston, Texas, kills more than 6,000.

1906 An earthquake and ensuing fire kills hundreds in San Francisco.

1919 The Great Boston Molasses Flood kills 21 and injures 150.

1925 A tornado kills nearly 700 in Illinois, Indiana, and Missouri.

1927 Floods cause devastation and social upheaval along the Mississippi River.

1933–1939 Drought and overfarming in the Southern Plains create "Dust Bowl" storms; displaced farmers leave Oklahoma, Texas, Kansas, and other states.

1937 The Ohio River reaches record flood levels.

1938 A hurricane strikes New York and New England.

1944 The Hartford, Connecticut, circus fire claims 168 lives.

Glossary of Archaic Occupations

accomptant accountant

aeronaut balloonist or a trapeze artist

alewife woman who keeps an alehouse or tavern

amanuensis secretary or stenographer

axle tree maker maker of axles for coaches and wagons

baxter baker

bluestocking female writer

brewster beer manufacturer

cohen priest

collier coal miner

cooper barrel-maker

costermonger fruit seller

couranteer journalist

crocker potter

gaoler jailer

hind farm laborer

huckster seller of small wares

husbandman tenant farmer

joyner/joiner skilled carpenter

lavender washer woman

leech/sawbones washer woman

pedascule schoolmaster

perambulator surveyor

peruker wigmaker

ratoner rat catcher

scappler person who roughly shapes stone in preparation for a mason

scutcher person who beats flax to soften the straw

slopseller seller of ready-made clothes

snobscat shoe repairer

tide waiter customs official

tie maker maker of wooden railway ties

tipstaff policeman

vulcan blacksmith

webster weaver

whitewing street sweeper

Glossary of Archaic Diseases

ablepsia blindness

acute angina sore throat

apoplexy paralyzed by stroke

bad blood, **Lues disease, French**, or **great pox** syphilis

biliousness jaundice caused by liver disease

black death, camp fever, or **ship's fever** typhus

brain fever meningitis

child bed fever infection following childbirth

cholelithiasis gallstones

congestive fever or **chills** malaria

consumption, African consumption, lung sickness, or **galloping consumption** tuberculosis

coryza or **catarrhal** cold or allergies

costiveness constipation

croup laryngitis, diphtheria, or strep throat

dengue infectious fever common in East Africa

dysentery diarrhea

dyspepsia heartburn, indigestion

falling sickness or **caduceus** epilepsy

fatty liver cirrhosis

fever 'n ague malarial fever

green sickness or **fever** anemia

grippe, grip, or **lagrippe** influenza (the flu)

infantile paralysis polio

lumbago back pain

lung or **winter fever** pneumonia

mormal gangrene

neuralgia general term for discomfort (e.g., "neuralgia in the head" is a headache)

puerperal exhaustion death due to childbirth

putrid fever, chin cough, bladder in throat, malignant sore throat, or **kruchhusten** diphtheria or whooping cough

quinsey tonsillitis

screws rheumatism

sugar diabetes insulin-dependent diabetes

thrush or **aphtha** childhood disease; spots on mouth, lips, and throat

Timeline of US Epidemics

1721 smallpox (New England)

1729 measles (Boston)

1738 smallpox (South Carolina)

1739–1740 measles (Boston)

1747 measles (Connecticut, New York, Pennsylvania, South Carolina)

1770s smallpox (Pacific Northwest)

1772 measles (North America)

1793–1798 yellow fever (recurs in Philadelphia)

1832 cholera (New York City, New Orleans, and other major cities)

1837 smallpox (Great Plains)

1837 typhus (Philadelphia)

1841 yellow fever (southern states)

1847 yellow fever (New Orleans)

1849 cholera (New York City; New Orleans, St. Louis and other cities along the Mississippi River)

1850 influenza (nationwide)

1851 cholera (Great Plains)

1852 yellow fever (nationwide, especially New Orleans)

1853 yellow fever (New Orleans)

1855 yellow fever (nationwide)

1860–1861 smallpox (Pennsylvania)

1862 smallpox (Pacific Northwest)

1865–1873 typhoid, yellow fever, scarlet fever (nationwide)

1865–1873 cholera (Baltimore, Memphis, Washington, DC)

1867 yellow fever (New Orleans)

1873–1875 influenza (nationwide)

1876 smallpox (South Dakota)

1878 yellow fever (lower Mississippi River valley)

1885 typhoid (Pennsylvania)

1886 yellow fever (Jacksonville, Florida)

1900–1904 "Third Pandemic" (San Francisco)

1916 polio (nationwide)

1918 Spanish influenza (worldwide)

1949 polio (nationwide)

1952 polio (nationwide)

Gregorian Calendar
Adoption Dates by Country

When the Gregorian calendar was introduced in 1582, it corrected math discrepancies in the old Julian calendar by dropping 10 days. That means you may need to adjust ancestors' birth and death dates that occurred before their countries adopted the new calendar.

COUNTRY	DATE OF ADOPTION
Alaska	Oct. 18, 1867
British Empire (including American colonies)	Sept. 14, 1752
Denmark (including Norway and some German states)	March 1, 1700 (solar portion) 1776 (lunar portion)
Dutch Republic	• Brabant, Zeeland, and Staten-Generaal: Dec. 25, 1582 • Gelderland: July 1700 • Overijssel and Utrecht: December 1700 • Friesland and Groningen: January 1701
France	Dec. 20, 1582
Greece	Feb. 15, 1923
Holland	Jan. 12, 1583
Italy	Oct. 15, 1582
Polish-Lithuanian Commonwealth	Oct. 15, 1582
Portugal	Oct. 15, 1582*
Prussia	Sept. 2, 1610
Russia	Feb. 14, 1918
Southern Netherlands (including modern Belgium)	Jan. 1, 1583
Sweden (including Finland)	March 1, 1753
Spain	Oct. 15, 1582*

* Spanish and Portuguese colonies adopted the new calendar later than their mother countries because of slow communications.

14

PHOTOGRAPHY

Historical Photo Formats

DAGUERREOTYPE (1839-C.1865)
A photo developed on a copper plate coated with highly polished silver, usually encased with a mat behind glass. You must hold the image at an angle to view it.

AMBROTYPE (1852-C.1870)
An image developed on glass backed with a dark varnish, cloth, or paper. You can often see through the image where the backing has deteriorated.

TINTYPE (MID-1850S-PRESENT)
Also known as a ferrotype or melainotype, the image was developed on a thin, blackened iron sheet coated with photo chemicals. The protective varnish may have darkened; the image also may rust.

CALOTYPE (1841-C.1862)
This early paper image, also called a talbotype, was common in England. The image may look fuzzy due to being printed with a paper negative. A salted paper print is a type of calotype with a clearer image. For both, the image appears to be embedded in the paper; a watermark may be visible.

ALBUMEN PRINT (1850-EARLY 1900S)
Developed from a glass negative on paper coated with egg whites and ammonium chloride, these images often were mounted onto thick paper to create 2.5x4-inch cartes des visite, and later, larger cabinet cards.

STEREOGRAPH (1854–1938)

Two nearly identical images mounted side by side resulted in a 3-D image when viewed through a stereoscope. A stereograph may be a daguerreotype or card photograph.

BLACK-AND-WHITE SNAPSHOTS (LATE 1880S–PRESENT)

The first amateur cameras were pre-loaded with film; the operator returned the camera to the factory to obtain prints and more film. The small prints were mounted on cardstock in a variety of sizes.

POSTCARD (1900–PRESENT)

Photos developed on paper pre-printed with a postcard back could be mailed to family and friends.

AUTOCHROME (1904–C. 1937)

These first commercially successful color pictures employed dyed vegetable starch to create color images on glass slides.

COLOR PAPER PRINTS (1941–PRESENT)

A negative image forms a positive color image when exposed onto photographic paper. Most are made from 35mm film.

POLAROID (1947–PRESENT)

A black-and-white or color image develops immediately after the film is exposed. Early on, the picture developed inside the camera and required a fixing agent. Later, the operator peeled away a backing to reveal the image; modern integral film enclosed photo chemicals inside a plastic packet.

6 Photo Preservation Tips

1. **Don't stick anything to the surface of an image**. Never laminate photos.

2. **Never write on the front of a photo**. Instead, write gently on the backs of old images with a soft lead pencil. For modern, plastic-coated papers, use a pen that's odorless when dry, waterproof, quick-drying. and fade-resistant (available in craft- and art-supply stores).

3. **Print digital images on photographic paper**. If you print images at home, make them last as long as possible by using a good photo printer and photographic (not regular office) paper.

4. **Use good-quality storage materials**. Keep old prints and cased images in acid-free, lignin-free boxes and envelopes. Albums also should be acid- and lignin-free; never the "magnetic" kind with adhesive pages. Mount photos with photo corners, not glue. Find supplies at photo and craft stores, and online retailers (run a web search on archival storage).

5. **Store photos in a cool, dry, dark location**. Exposure to high humidity, temperature extremes, and light can cause discoloration and deterioration. Keep photos in a living area of your home, away from fireplaces and other heat sources. A shelf in an interior closet is ideal.

6. **Scan and make copies of photos for display**, rather than displaying the originals. Keep a high-resolution, TIFF-format preservation copy of each digitized photo, and make another copy for editing, viewing, and sharing. Back up your digital images in multiple places.

6 Photo ID Tips

1. **Share the mystery photo with relatives.** You can scan and e-mail pictures, mail copies, or visit your relatives and deliver photos in person. Ask what your relatives know about who's in the photo, and when and where it was taken. Also ask if they have similar photos.

2. **Determine the format of the photo** (daguerreotype? tintype? postcard?) to help you narrow the date is was taken. A stamp box on the back of a postcard can help you narrow the date even more.

3. **Examine clothing, hairstyles, and props in the photo**, and consult a resource such as *The Family Photo Detective* by Maureen A. Taylor (Family Tree Books, 2013) to learn when those styles were popular.

4. **Magnify and study small background details** by scanning the image at a high resolution (600 dpi or more) and enlarging it on your computer screen. You also can use a photographer's loupe to magnify details. Look for clues about the photo's location and the occasion.

5. **Estimate the ages of people and compare them** to your paper research. For example, look for families in which the number, sex, and ages of the children fit what you see in the photograph.

6. **Examine facial features in photos**. Are you trying to determine whether people in a group photo are related? Want to determine whether two photos show the same person? Look to the person's face (especially the face shape, eyes, ears, and nose) for similarities.

Photography

Sources of Family Photographs

Missing some faces from your photo collection?
One of these resources may have the image you seek:

- relatives
- family friends
- local historical society and library collections
- photo-reunion websites (such as DeadFred **<www.deadfred.com>** and AncientFaces **<www.ancientfaces.com>**)
- driver's and other licenses
- employment or military IDs
- newsletters for employers, clubs, or fraternal organizations
- school yearbooks
- newspapers
- naturalization records
- immigrant identification cards
- passports
- criminal records
- mugbooks
- marriage certificates
- local and county histories
- published genealogies
- town and church centennial books
- biographical directories
- church membership directories
- eBay **<www.ebay.com>** and other auction websites

Writing Photo Captions

When you caption your family photos—whether they're old black-and-white pictures or the snapshots you took just yesterday—include as much as you know of this information:

- full name(s) of the person or people pictured
- dates of birth and death of the person or people pictured
- name of the photographer
- date the photo was taken
- occasion or event shown
- place where the photo was taken
- provenance of the image: names of the original owner and those who've owned it since (or a source citation, if you found the image in a repository's collection or on a website)
- your name
- your relationship to the people pictured

Photo-Editing Tools

Are you restoring digitized family photos? If your photo-editing software's autocorrect feature doesn't do the job, here's a rundown of the tools you may use:

airbrush The airbrush tool simulates an actual airbrush or spray-paint can when applying a color. The longer you hold the airbrush over the image, the greater the effect. Airbrush options include the size and shape of the brush, as well as the spray's intensity.

blur This tool softens portions of an image so they appear slightly out of focus, obscuring imperfections.

burn The burn tool is the opposite of Dodge: It darkens areas of the image that are too light.

clone (or rubber stamp) The clone tool does exactly what it implies: It replicates good areas of an image, so you can hide damaged areas. The source (the "good" area) can be from the same photo or an entirely different one.

dodge This lightens too-dark areas and brings out detail. Dodge takes its name from the traditional darkroom technique of holding back some of the light when printing a photo.

red-eye reduction This tool helps you get rid of the red-eye effect often caused by flash photography.

smudge Smudge softens an image by smearing details (rather than lightening the color, as the Blur tool does). Smudge is great for tackling tiny imperfections.

Digital Photo Resolution Guide

For best results when scanning your family photos, refer to this chart and set the resolution according to how you plan to use the digitized image.

Intended Use	Resolution (dots per inch)	Size (in pixels)	Best file format
Photo prints	300 dpi (Use a higher dpi if you plan to enlarge the photo)	1,200x1,800 (minimum)	JPG
Posting on website	72 dpi	640x800	JPG
E-mailing	72 dpi	640x800 (maximum, unless recipient plans to print)	JPG
Archiving negatives or slides	Scan at highest optical resolution of the scanner (at least 1,200 dpi)	Varies, depending on size of original and scanner capability	TIFF or JPG
Archiving photos	300 dpi	1,200 x 1,800 (minimum)	TIFF or JPG

Photography

WORKSHEETS

As you dive deeper into your family's history, the amount of information you find can be overwhelming. Use the worksheets in this section to help you organize and share your family tree data.

In this section, you'll find:

- **Family Group Sheet:** Save information about a single-family unit.
- **Ancestor Worksheet:** Record a host of information about one individual family member.
- **Five-Generation Ancestor Chart:** Document your family back to your great-great-grandparents.
- **Research Repository Worksheet:** Plan trips to archives, cemeteries, and other record-holding locations.
- **Source Citation Worksheet:** Track where you got your research with this template for recording information about your sources.
- **Surname Variant Worksheet:** Save time in your research by listing the different ways your ancestor's name could be spelled in records.
- **DNA Cousin Match Worksheet:** Manage your most important DNA matches with this quick-reference sheet.

Family Group Sheet

of the _____ Family

Husband   Source #

Full name _____   _____

Birth date _____ Place _____   _____

Marriage date _____ Place _____   _____

Death date _____ Place _____   _____

　　　Burial _____   _____

His father _____   _____

His mother with maiden name _____   _____

Wife

Full name _____   _____

Birth date _____ Place _____   _____

Death date _____ Place _____   _____

　　　Burial _____   _____

Her father _____   _____

Her mother with maiden name _____   _____

Other Spouses

Full name _____   _____

　　　Marriage date and place _____   _____

Full name _____   _____

　　　Marriage date and place _____   _____

Children of this marriage	Birth date and place	Death and burial dates and places	Spouse and marriage date and place

WORKSHEETS **205**

Ancestor Worksheet

Full Name (maiden name for women): _____

Social Security Number: _____

Nicknames and Alternate Names: _____

Surname Spelling Variations: _____

Birth and Baptism

Birth Date: _____ Birth Place: _____

Baptism Date: _____ Baptism Place: _____

Marriage(s) and Divorce(s)

Name of Spouse(s)	Marriage Date(s)	Marriage Place(s)

Name of Spouse(s)	Divorce Date(s)	Divorce Place(s)

Death

Death Date: _____ Death Place: _____

Burial Date: _____ Burial Church/Place: _____

Obituary Date(s) and Newspaper(s): _____

Military Service

Conflict (if applicable)	Unit	Dates/Years

Migration

From	To	Departure/ Arrival Dates	Companion(s)	Ship (if applicable)

Personal Information

Schools Attended: _____

Religion Church(es) Attended: _____

Hobbies Club Memberships: _____

Children

Child's Name	Birth Date	Birthplace	Other Parent

Friends, Witnesses, and Neighbors to Research

Name	Relationship

Five-Generation Ancestor Chart

4

birth date and place

marriage date and place

death date and place

2

birth date and place

marriage date and place

death date and place

5

birth date and place

death date and place

1

birth date and place

marriage date and place

death date and place

spouse

6

birth date and place

marriage date and place

death date and place

3

birth date and place

death date and place

7

birth date and place

death date and place

Chart # ___

1 on this chart = ___ on chart # ___

see chart #

16

8 _____

17

birth date and place _____

marriage date and place _____

death date and place _____

18

9 _____

19

birth date and place _____

death date and place _____

20

10 _____

21

birth date and place _____

marriage date and place _____

death date and place _____

22

11 _____

23

birth date and place _____

death date and place _____

24

12 _____

25

birth date and place _____

marriage date and place _____

death date and place _____

26

13 _____

27

birth date and place _____

death date and place _____

28

14 _____

29

birth date and place _____

marriage date and place _____

death date and place _____

30

15 _____

31

birth date and place _____

death date and place _____

Research Repository Worksheet

Name of repository: _____

Address/Directions	
Hours (Closed for Lunch?)	
Holidays closed	
Name of contact person	
Cost of photocopies	
Restrictions on photocopying	
Change machine or cashier?	
Nearest places to park (with cost)	
Nearest places to eat	
Local lodging	
Handicap access?	
Research restrictions (Briefcases/laptops allowed? Lockers available?	
Any records stored off site? If so, how can they be accessed?	

Source Citation Worksheet

Source type (book, manuscript, type of record, etc.)	
Source format (microfilm, original, printed copy, etc.)	
Author or creator's name (agency, department, person)	
Title of work	
Date of work	
Publication place and publisher	
Collection or series name	
Box and folder	
Page number	
Repository	
Date viewed	
Notes on condition	

Surname Variant Worksheet

Surname			
Place of origin			
Phonetic variants			
Possible variations into English			
Surname suffixes (-son, -datter, etc.)			
Other spellings/ variants			

DNA Cousin Match Worksheet

Percentage Match	Centimorgans (CM)	Relationship	Notes

YOUR FREQUENTLY CITED FACTS

This book contains the genealogy facts and figures that are likely to be useful to most US-based researchers. But each genealogist's research is different, and you'll undoubtedly need quick access to details specific to your family history: dates, statistics, names, foreign-language words, and facts about your ancestor's life and times.

To help you organize all these statistics, we've included this section where you can record your own frequently cited facts. Simply fill the following pages with key information you'd like to have available at a glance, such as:

- spelling variations for your ancestor's name or hometown
- nicknames or aliases your ancestors were known to have gone by
- birth, immigration, marriage, and death dates and places for key research subjects (grandparents, great-grandparents, etc.)
- timelines of your ancestor's life
- notes about the history of your ancestor's hometown
- lists of foreign-language vocabulary that you frequently find in records
- genealogy websites you often traffic, or brick-and-mortar records archives you want to visit in person
- citation information, such as microfilm numbers

Other Family Tree Books are available from your local bookstore and online suppliers. For more genealogy resources, visit **<familytreemagazine.com/store>**.

22 21 20 19 18   5 4 3 2 1

DISTRIBUTED IN THE U.K. AND EUROPE BY
F&W Media International, LTD
Brunel House, Forde Close,
Newton Abbot, TQ12 4PU, UK
Tel: (+44) 1626 323200,
Fax (+44) 1626 323319
E-mail: enquiries@fwmedia.com

a content + ecommerce company

PUBLISHER AND COMMUNITY LEADER: Allison Dolan
EDITOR: Andrew Koch
DESIGNER: Julie Barnett
PRODUCTION COORDINATOR: Debbie Thomas

223

4 FREE Family Tree Templates

- decorative family tree posters
- five-generation ancestor chart
- family group sheet
- relationship chart
- type and save, or print and fill out

Download at <www.familytreemagazine.com/familytreefreebies>

MORE GREAT GENEALOGY RESOURCES

ORGANIZE YOUR GENEALOGY

By Drew Smith

UNOFFICIAL ANCESTRY.COM WORKBOOK

By Nancy Hendrickson

STORY OF MY LIFE:
A Journal For Preserving Your Legacy

By Sunny Jane Morton

Available from your favorite bookstore, online booksellers
and <familytreemagazine.com/store>, or by calling (855) 278-0408.

Join our community! <facebook.com/familytreemagazine>